THOMAS SMALLWOOD

# The Writings of Thomas Smallwood

*Edited with an Introduction and Notes by*
SCOTT SHANE

*General Editor:*
HENRY LOUIS GATES, JR.

PENGUIN BOOKS

PENGUIN BOOKS

An imprint of Penguin Random House LLC
1745 Broadway, New York, NY 10019
penguinrandomhouse.com



Set in Sabon LT Pro

LIBRARY OF CONGRESS CATALOGING-IN-PUBLICATION DATA
Names: Smallwood, Thomas, 1801–1883 author | Shane, Scott, 1954– editor |
Smallwood, Thomas, 1801–1883. A narrative of Thomas Smallwood (Coloured man)
Title: The writings of Thomas Smallwood / Thomas Smallwood ;
edited with an introduction and notes by Scott Shane.
Description: New York, NY : Penguin Books, [2026] | Contains the "Sam Weller" Letters and A Narrative of Thomas Smallwood. | Includes bibliographical references.
Identifiers: LCCN 2025023692 | ISBN 9780143138389 paperback |
ISBN 9780593512432 ebook
Subjects: LCSH: Smallwood, Thomas, 1801–1883 | African American abolitionists—Biography | Abolitionists—United States—Biography | Underground Railroad | Torrey, Charles T. (Charles Turner), 1813–1846 | Toronto (Ont.)—Biography
Classification: LCC E450.S59 A3 2026
LC record available at https://lccn.loc.gov/2025023692

Printed in the United States of America
1st Printing

The authorized representative in the EU for product safety and compliance is Penguin Random House Ireland, Morrison Chambers, 32 Nassau Street, Dublin D02 YH68, Ireland, https://eu-contact.penguin.ie.

# Contents



## THE WRITINGS OF THOMAS SMALLWOOD

# What Is an African American Classic?

I have long nurtured a deep and abiding affection for the Penguin Classics, at least since I was an undergraduate at Yale. I used to imagine that my attraction for these books—grouped together, as a set, in some independent bookstores when I was a student, and perhaps even in some today—stemmed from the fact that my first-grade classmates, for some reason that I can't recall, were required to dress as penguins in our annual all-school pageant, and perform a collective side-to-side motion that our misguided teacher thought she could choreograph into something meant to pass for a "dance." Piedmont, West Virginia, in 1956, was a very long way from Penguin Nation, wherever that was supposed to be! But penguins we were determined to be, and we did our level best to avoid wounding each other with our orange-colored cardboard beaks while stomping out of rhythm in our matching orange, veined webbed feet. The whole scene was madness, one never to be repeated at the Davis Free School. But I never stopped loving penguins. And I have never stopped loving the very audacity of the idea of the Penguin Classics, an affordable, accessible library of the most important and compelling texts in the history of civilization, their uniform spines and type and alluring covers giving each text a comfortable, familiar feel, as if we have encountered it, or its cousins, before. I think of the Penguin Classics as the very best and most compelling in human thought, an Alexandrian library in paperback, enclosed in black and white.

I still gravitate to the Penguin Classics when killing time in an airport bookstore, deferring the slow torture of the security lines. Sometimes I even purchase two or three, fantasizing that

I can speed-read one of the shorter titles, then make a dent in the longer one, vainly attempting to fill the holes in the liberal arts education that our degrees suggest we have, over the course of a plane ride! Mark Twain once quipped that a classic is "something that everybody wants to have read and nobody wants to read," and perhaps that applies to my airport purchasing habits. For my generation, these titles in the Penguin Classics form the canon—the canon of the texts that a truly well-educated person should have read, and read carefully and closely, at least once. For years I rued the absence of texts by Black authors in this series, and longed to be able to make even a small contribution to the diversification of this astonishingly universal list. I watched with great pleasure as titles by African American and African authors began to appear, some two dozen over the past several years. So when Vice President and Publisher Elda Rotor approached me about editing a series of African American classics and collections for Penguin's Portable Series, I eagerly accepted.

Thinking about the titles appropriate for inclusion in these series led me, inevitably, to think about what, for me, constitutes a "classic." And thinking about this led me, in turn, to the wealth of reflections on what defines a work of literature or philosophy somehow speaking to the human condition beyond time and place, a work somehow endlessly compelling, generation upon generation, a work whose author we don't have to look like to identify with, to feel at one with, as we find ourselves transported through the magic of a textual time machine; a work that refracts the image of ourselves that we project onto it, regardless of our ethnicity, our gender, our time, our place. This is what centuries of scholars and writers have meant when they use the word *classic*, and—despite all that we know about the complex intersubjectivity of the production of meaning in the wondrous exchange between a reader and a text—it remains true that classic texts, even in the most conventional, conservative sense of the word *classic*, do exist, and these books will continue to be read long after the generation the text reflects and defines, the generation of readers contemporary with the text's author, is dead and gone.

Classic texts speak from their authors' graves, in their names, in their voices. As Italo Calvino once remarked, "A classic is a book that has never finished saying what it has to say."

Faulkner put this idea in an interesting way: "The aim of every artist is to arrest motion, which is life, by artificial means, and hold it fixed so that a hundred years later, when a stranger looks at it, it moves again since it is life." That, I am certain, must be the desire of every writer. But what about the reader? What makes a book a classic to a reader? Here, perhaps, Hemingway said it best: "All good books are alike in that they are truer than if they had really happened and after you are finished reading one you will feel that all that happened to you, and afterward it belongs to you, the good and the bad, the ecstasy, the remorse and sorrow, the people and the places and how the weather was."

I have been reading Black literature since I was fifteen, yanked into the dark discursive universe by an Episcopal priest at a church camp near my home in West Virginia in August 1965, during the terrifying days of the Watts Riots in Los Angeles. Eventually, by fits and starts, studying the literature written by Black authors became my avocation; ultimately, it has become my vocation. And, in my own way, I have tried to be an evangelist for it, to a readership larger than my own people, people who, as it were, look like these texts. Here, I am reminded of something W. S. Merwin said about the books he most loved: "Perhaps a classic is a work that one imagines should be common knowledge, but more and more often isn't." I would say, of African and African American literature, that perhaps classic works by Black writers are works that one imagines should be common knowledge among the broadest possible readership but that less and less are, as the teaching of reading to understand how words can create the worlds into which books can transport us yields to classroom instruction geared toward passing a state-authorized standardized exam. All literary texts suffer from this wrongheaded approach to teaching, mind you; but it especially affects texts by people of color, and texts by women—texts still struggling, despite enormous gains over the last twenty years, to gain a solid foothold in anthologies and syllabi. For every anthology, every syllabus, every publishing series such as the Penguin Classics constitutes a distinct "canon," an implicit definition of all that is essential for a truly educated person to read.

James Baldwin, who has pride of place in my personal canon of African American authors since it was one of his books that that Episcopal priest gave me to read in that dreadful summer of 1965, argued that "the responsibility of a writer is to excavate the experience of the people who produced him." But surely Baldwin would have agreed with E. M. Forster that the books that we remember, the books that have truly influenced us, are those that "have gone a little further down our particular path than we have yet ourselves." Excavating the known is a worthy goal of the writer as cultural archeologist; yet, at the same time, so is unveiling the unknown, the unarticulated yet shared experience of the colorless things that make us human: "Something we have always known (or thought we knew)," as Calvino puts it, "but without knowing that this author said it first." We might think of the difference between Forster and Baldwin, on the one hand, and Calvino, on the other, as the difference between an author representing what has happened (Forster, Baldwin) in the history of a people whose stories, whose very history itself, has long been suppressed, and what could have happened (Calvino) in the atemporal realm of art. This is an important distinction when thinking about the nature of an African American classic—rather, when thinking about the nature of the texts that constitute the African American literary tradition or, for that matter, the texts in any under-read tradition.

One of James Baldwin's most memorable essays, a subtle meditation on sexual preference, race, and gender, is entitled "Here Be Dragons." So much of traditional African American literature, even fiction and poetry—ostensibly at least once removed from direct statement—was meant to deal a fatal blow to the dragon of racism. For Black writers since the eighteenth-century beginnings of the tradition, literature has been one more weapon—a very important weapon, mind you, but still one weapon among many—in the arsenal Black people have drawn upon to fight against antiblack racism and for their equal rights before the law. Ted Joans, the Black surrealist poet, called this sort of literature from the sixties' Black Arts Movement "hand grenade poems." Of what possible use are the niceties of figuration when one must slay a dragon? I can hear you say, give me the blunt weapon anytime! Problem is, it is more difficult than some writers seem to think to slay a dragon with a poem or a novel. Social problems persist; literature too tied to addressing those social problems tends to enter the historical archives, leaving the realm of the literary. Let me state bluntly what should be obvious: Writers are read for how they write, not what they write about.

Frederick Douglass—for this generation of readers one of the most widely read writers—reflected on this matter even in the midst of one of his most fiery speeches addressing the ironies of the sons and daughters of slaves celebrating the Fourth of July while slavery continued unabated. In his now-classic speech "What to the Slave Is the Fourth of July?" (1852), Douglass argued that an immediate, almost transparent form of discourse was demanded of Black writers by the heated temper of the times, a discourse with an immediate end in mind: "At a time like this, scorching irony, not convincing argument, is needed . . . a fiery stream of biting ridicule, blasting reproach, withering sarcasm, and stern rebuke. For it is not light that is needed, but fire; it is not the gentle shower, but thunder. We need the storm, the whirlwind, and the earthquake." Above all else, Douglass concludes, the rhetoric of the literature created by African Americans must, of necessity, be a purposeful rhetoric, its ends targeted at attacking the evils that afflict Black people: "The feeling of the nation must be quickened; the conscience of the nation must be roused; the propriety of the nation must be startled; the hypocrisy of the nation must be exposed; and its crimes against God and man must be proclaimed and denounced." And perhaps this was so; nevertheless, we read Douglass's writings today in literature classes not so much for their content but to understand, and marvel at, his sublime mastery of words, words—to paraphrase Calvino—that never finish saying what it is they have to say, not because of their "message" but because of the language in which that message is inextricably enfolded.

There are as many ways to define a classic in the African American tradition as there are in any other tradition, and these ways are legion. So many essays have been published entitled "What Is a Classic?" that they could fill several large anthologies. And while no one can say explicitly why generations of readers return to read certain texts, just about everyone can agree that making a bestseller list in one's lifetime is most certainly not an index of fame or influence over time; the longevity of one's readership—of books about which one says, "I am rereading," as Calvino puts it—on the other hand, most certainly is. So, the size of one's readership (through library use, Internet access, and sales) cumulatively is an interesting factor to consider; and because of series such as the Penguin Classics, we can gain a sense, for our purposes, of those texts written by authors in previous generations that have sustained sales—mostly for classroom use—long after their authors were dead.

There can be little doubt that *Narrative of the Life of Frederick Douglass* (1845), *The Souls of Black Folk* (1903) by W. E. B. Du Bois, and *Their Eyes Were Watching God* (1937) by Zora Neale Hurston, are three of the most classic of the Black classics—again, as measured by consumption—while Langston Hughes's poetry, though not purchased as books in these large numbers, is accessed online as frequently as that of any other American poet, and indeed profoundly more so than most. Within Penguin Classics, the most popular individual titles, excluding Douglass's first slave narrative and Du Bois's *Souls*, include:

*The Interesting Narrative* (1789), Olaudah Equiano
*My Bondage and My Freedom* (1855), Frederick Douglass
*The Light of Truth* (2014), Ida B. Wells
*Quicksand* (1928), Nella Larsen
*Passing* (1929), Nella Larsen
*Black No More* (1931), George Schuyler
*The River Between* (1965), Ngũgĩ wa Thiong'o
*The Cancer Journals* (1980), Audre Lorde

*Sister Outsider* (1984), Audre Lorde
*The African Trilogy* (2010), Chinua Achebe
*Romance in Marseille* (2020), Claude McKay

These titles form a canon of classic African American literature, judged by classroom readership. If we add Jean Toomer's novel *Cane* (1923), arguably the first work of African American modernism, along with Douglass's first narrative, Du Bois's *Souls*, and Hurston's *Their Eyes*, we would most certainly have included many of the touchstones of Black literature published before 1940, when Richard Wright published *Native Son*.

Every teacher's syllabus constitutes a canon of sorts, and I teach these texts and a few others as the classics of the Black canon. Why these particular texts? I can think of two reasons: First, these texts signify or riff upon each other, repeating, borrowing, and extending metaphors book to book, generation to generation. To take just a few examples, Equiano's eighteenth-century use of the trope of the talking book (an image found, remarkably, in five slave narratives published between 1770 and 1811) becomes, with Frederick Douglass, the representation of the quest for freedom as, necessarily, the quest for literacy, for a freedom larger than physical manumission; we might think of this as the representation of metaphysical manumission, of freedom and literacy—the literacy of great literature—inextricably intertwined. Douglass transformed the metaphor of the talking book into the trope of chiasmus, a repetition with a stinging reversal: "You have seen how a man becomes a slave, you will see how a slave becomes a man." Du Bois, with Douglass very much on his mind, transmuted chiasmus a half century later into the metaphor of duality or double consciousness, a necessary condition of living one's life, as he memorably put it, behind a "veil."

Du Bois's metaphor has a powerful legacy in twentieth-century Black fiction: James Weldon Johnson, in *The Autobiography of an Ex-Colored Man* (1912), literalizes the trope of double consciousness by depicting as his protagonist a man who, at will, can occupy two distinct racial spaces, one Black, one white, and who moves seamlessly, if ruefully, between them; Toomer's *Cane* takes Du Bois's metaphor of duality for the inevitably split consciousness that every Negro must feel living in a country in which her or his status as a citizen is liminal at best, or has been erased at worst, and makes of this the metaphor for the human condition itself under modernity, a tellingly bold rhetorical gesture—one designed to make the Negro the metaphor of the human condition. And Hurston, in *Their Eyes*, extends Toomer's revision even further, depicting a character who can gain her voice only once she can name this condition of duality or double consciousness and then glide gracefully and lyrically between her two selves, an "inside" self and an "outside" one.

More recently, Alice Walker, in *The Color Purple* (1982), signifies upon two aspects of the narrative strategy of *Their Eyes*: First, she revisits the theme of a young Black woman finding her voice, depicting a protagonist who writes herself into being through letters addressed to God and to her sister, Nettie—letters that grow ever more sophisticated in their syntax and grammar and imagery as she comes to consciousness before our very eyes, letter to letter; and second, Walker riffs on Hurston's use of a vernacular-inflected free indirect discourse to show that Black English has the capacity to serve as the medium for narrating a novel through the Black dialect that forms a most pliable and expansive language in Celie's letters. Ralph Ellison makes Du Bois's metaphor of the veil a trope of blindness and life underground for his protagonist in *Invisible Man* (1952), a protagonist who, as he types the story of his life from a hole underground, writes himself into being in the first person (in contradistinction to Richard Wright's protagonist, Bigger Thomas, whose reactive tale of fear and flight is told in the third person). Walker's novel also riffs on Ellison's claim for the revolutionary possibilities of writing the self into being, whereas Hurston's protagonist, Janie, speaks herself into being. Ellison himself signified multiply upon Richard Wright's *Native Son*, from the title to the use of the first-person bildungsroman to chart the coming to consciousness of a sensitive protagonist moving from blindness and an inability to do little more than react to his environment, to the insight gained by wresting control of his identity from social forces and strong individuals that would circumscribe and confine his life choices. Toni Morrison, master supernaturalist and perhaps the greatest Black novelist of all, trumps Ellison's trope of blindness by returning over and over to the possibilities and limits of insight within worlds confined or circumscribed not by supraforces (à la Wright) but by the confines of the imagination and the ironies of individual and family history, signifying upon Faulkner, Woolf, and García Márquez in the process. And Ishmael Reed, the father of Black postmodernism and what we might think of as the hip-hop novel, the tradition's master parodist, signifies upon everybody and everything in the Black literary tradition, from the slave narratives to the Harlem Renaissance to Black nationalism and feminism.

This sort of literary signifying is what makes a literary tradition, well, a "tradition," rather than a simple list of books whose authors happen to have been born in the same country, share the same gender, or would be identified by their peers as belonging to this ethnic group or that. What makes these books special—"classic"—however, is something else. Each text has the uncanny capacity to take the seemingly mundane details of the day-to-day African American experience of its time and transmute those details and the characters' actions into something that transcends its ostensible subject's time and place, its specificity. These texts reveal the human universal through the African American particular: All true art, all classics, do this; this is what "art" is, a revelation of that which makes each of us sublimely human, rendered in the minute details of the actions and thoughts and feelings of a compelling character embedded in a time and place. But as soon as we find ourselves turning to a text for its anthropological or sociological data, we have left the realm of art; we have reduced the complexity of fiction or poetry to an essay, and this is not what imaginative literature is for. Richard Wright, at his best, did this, as did his signifying disciple Ralph Ellison; Louis Armstrong and Duke Ellington, Bessie Smith and Billie

Holiday achieved this effect in music; Jacob Lawrence and Romare Bearden achieved it in the visual arts. And this is what Wole Soyinka does in his tragedies, what Toni Morrison does in her novels, what Derek Walcott did in his poetry. And while it is risky to name one's contemporaries in a list such as this, I think that Rita Dove and Jamaica Kincaid achieve this effect as well, as do Colson Whitehead and Edwidge Danticat, in a younger generation. (There are other writers whom I would include in this group had I the space.) By delving ever so deeply into the particularity of the African and African American experience, these authors manage, somehow, to come out the other side, making the race or the gender of their characters almost translucent, less important than the fact that they stand as aspects of ourselves beyond race or gender or time or place, precisely in the same magical way that Hamlet never remains for long stuck as a prince in a court in Denmark.

Each classic Black text reveals to us, uncannily, subtly, how the Black Experience is inscribed, inextricably and indelibly, in the human experience, and how the human experience takes one of its myriad forms in blackface, as it were. Together, such texts also demonstrate, implicitly, that African American culture is one of the world's truly great and eternal cultures, as noble and as resplendent as any. And it is to publish such texts, written by African and African American authors, that Penguin has created this series, which I have the pleasure of editing.

HENRY LOUIS GATES, JR.

# Introduction

In the early summer of 1842, Thomas Smallwood sat down and began to write himself into American literary history.[1] It was likely the middle of the night, in the little house on 4th Street in Southeast Washington, D.C., that he shared with his wife and four children. The house was just a stroll away from the United States Capitol, where the issue of slavery had Congress tied up in knots. Smallwood, forty-one, who had spent his first thirty years in slavery before purchasing his freedom, closely followed the bitter debates, but he had an eminently practical approach to the defining moral and political conflict of his time. At the end of long days running his shoemaking business, he was spending most of his nights organizing mass escapes from slavery.

All that was a lot to take on, but it wasn't enough for him. Smallwood, an avid reader who had educated himself to an astonishing standard without ever attending school, decided to write about the escapes, too. He had read widely in ancient and contemporary literature, and he was a devoted fan of Charles Dickens, whose rollicking *Pickwick Papers* had recently taken the reading world by storm.[2] Smallwood decided to attack the deadly serious subject of slavery with a Dickensian mix of acid, insight, irony, wit, and humor. He began to write an extraordinary series of dispatches for a little abolitionist newspaper in Albany,[3] New York, using the real names of local slaveholders in Washington, Baltimore, and the surrounding counties and the real names of the people he had helped to escape from them. But because he was engaged in a highly illegal, hugely dangerous activity—if caught, he might be killed on the spot, sent to prison for many years, or even returned to slavery—he could not sign his dispatches with his own name. He chose to call himself Samivel Weller,[4] the bootblack and manservant in *The Pickwick Papers* who was many readers' favorite character, paying tribute to Dickens and tapping into public affection for a fictional English servant who was wittier and wiser than his master.

Over the next sixteen months, he would send off a score of dispatches, displaying remarkable literary flair and range: hilarious satire, scathing condemnation, knowing exposé, somber reflection. His letters to Albany's *Tocsin of Liberty*, renamed *Albany Weekly Patriot* in early 1843, had one overriding purpose: to mock the slaveholders whose "walking property walked off,"[5] as Smallwood put it, and celebrate those who had escaped from them. But Smallwood, who seems to have been writing for publication for the first time, was a striking talent and clearly wanted to try out a range of styles and tones.

Smallwood's newspaper pieces are distinguished in multiple ways. They are a unique work of journalism, the only accounts of escapes from slavery by an organizer to be published in real time—he sometimes held a dispatch for a week to make sure the people named in it had safely reached Canada. Though fueled by outrage, they are a rare attempt to use satire and comedy against the slave power, as abolitionists in his day called it. The dispatches turn the social order upside down, with Smallwood wielding his "lash"—as he calls his pen—against the enslavers, the slave traders, and the slave-catching police. To rub salt into the enslavers' wounds, Smallwood insisted that the editors in Albany send a copy of the newspaper to every slaveholder he named in his dispatches.

When an angry slaveholder speculated publicly that this "Samivel Weller" who was causing such trouble might be Charles Torrey, the young Massachusetts abolitionist who helped Smallwood with the early escapes, Smallwood's glee was uncontainable. "The ignorant blunderhead!"[6] he fumed in mock indignation. "Is not *my* name carried to the world's end? Am I to be confounded with an obscure abolitionist, and *he* to be persecuted for my misdeeds!" He added his most concise description of the literary job he had assigned to himself: "I, Samivel Weller, jr. will continue to SCOFF at, *annoy*, and *expose* the slaveholders, and their crooked ways, to their perfect mystification and great pain, during weeks and months to come! The ignoramuses! to think to catch *such* a weasel as I, asleep."

And as Smallwood cast about for new ways to throttle his enemies in print, he seized upon a sardonic phrase evidently being passed around among the slave catchers baffled by the proliferation of mass escapes, many of them organized by Smallwood: *underground railroad*. In his newspaper pieces, Smallwood reported[7] that a notorious Baltimore police constable and slave catcher, John Zell, had been overheard grumbling that the enslaved must be getting away by "under ground rail-road" or "steam balloon." (There were no underground railroads, and steam balloons were experimental, so Zell was using colorful language to say he had no idea how so many people were escaping.)

Smallwood was the first writer to use the phrase in print (in his dispatch printed August 10, 1842), and, delighted by this backhanded compliment to those fleeing north and their helpers, he wielded it repeatedly to ridicule his foes. He earnestly advised enslavers in search of their lost human property to inquire at the (nonexistent) office of the underground railroad in Washington. He gave himself, with mock grandiosity, a splendid title: "general agent of all the branches of the National Underground Railroad, Steam Packet, Canal and Foot-it Company."[8] Other writers picked up "underground railroad" from him, and by the mid-1840s it became standard shorthand for escapes, especially those aided by others, gradually losing its sarcastic sting.

Smallwood operated in the same Chesapeake region that produced the biggest names in the battle against slavery. He began organizing mass escapes from D.C., Baltimore, and their suburbs some seven years before Harriet Tubman fled a plantation on Maryland's Eastern Shore, where she would return repeatedly to lead others north. He began writing about slavery in his Albany dispatches three years before Frederick Douglass published the first of his autobiographies, which described how he had dressed as a sailor and escaped Baltimore by train.

Such facts pose an obvious question: Why is Thomas Smallwood, who (with help from Charles Torrey and others) liberated between two hundred and four hundred people from bondage, wrote brilliant satirical attacks on the institution of slavery, and gave the underground railroad its name, not better known? It was a question that troubled me as I was writing *Flee North: A Forgotten Hero and the Fight for Freedom in Slavery's Borderland*, my 2023 book that featured Smallwood as its central character. The answer is complex and painful, best considered after we review his life and work.

By his own account, Thomas Smallwood was born on February 22, 1801, in Bladensburg, Maryland, a small town in Prince George's County, about six miles northeast of the United States Capitol. In the memoir he would publish a half century later, he says nothing about his parents, a possible indication that he was separated from them at an early age, a common fate among the enslaved. But Thomas and his sister, Catharine, called Kitty, had the good fortune to be inherited by Sarah Ferguson, who in 1808 married a local minister, the Rev. John Bell Ferguson. John Ferguson was "no friend to slavery," in Smallwood's words, and he bought Thomas and his sister from his new wife and her children—whether children by Ferguson or by a previous husband is unclear. In 1815, he signed a manumission document committing to free Thomas in fifteen years, at the age of thirty, while he separately advised Thomas that he would have to repay the $500 Ferguson had paid for him. (Ferguson's math was off, it appears, since Thomas by his own reckoning had not quite turned fourteen when the document was filed at the Prince George's County courthouse.)

John and Sarah Ferguson taught Thomas to read, making him a sort of neighborhood celebrity, and the Fergusons soon moved to Southeast Washington, settling near the Navy Yard. As a young man, Smallwood hugely expanded his self-education while working as a household servant for a Scottish-born Washington educator, John McLeod. Smallwood writes that McLeod and his adult children encouraged him in his reading, and by the time he received his freedom, he had an impressive command of classical and contemporary literature, history, and politics.

His growing knowledge of the world drew him in his early twenties to the colonization movement, which aided free African Americans in moving to Liberia, the new country in West Africa founded by the American Colonization Society. Two close friends moved to Liberia, and Smallwood for a time imagined that the best way to escape American laws and prejudices might be to abandon America. But by the time he was free, about 1830, he had come to the realization that many white supporters of colonization viewed the movement as a way to preserve slavery. He declared himself "grievously deceived" by the colonizationists: "Said they, if we can get rid of the free negro population we can put a stop to any further emancipations, and thus have perpetual slavery without danger."[9]

Smallwood had married a free Virginia woman, Elizabeth Anderson, and by the time he was forty, in 1841, they had four children. He'd been free for a decade, and he seemed to be thriving in the shoemaker's trade. But his disillusionment with colonization did not alter his desire to confront the institution of slavery, which he despised.

By Smallwood's reckoning, the catalyst he needed arrived in Washington at the end of 1841. Charles Turner Torrey was a white Massachusetts abolitionist a dozen years younger than Smallwood. Though his parents and sister had died of tuberculosis when he was small, he had been raised in the house of his grandfather, who had served in Congress and was a respected public figure. Charles was sent to Exeter and Yale.

But his fine education did not lead to a smooth start in life. He tried his hand at schoolteaching and preaching but failed quite spectacularly at both before discovering his passion: the antislavery movement. By 1839, Torrey was in the middle of a fight over the direction of New England's abolition movement, seeking with a few allies to topple its leader, William Lloyd Garrison. Torrey and his friends particularly faulted Garrison's quixotic belief that the political and electoral system were too corrupted by slavery to be useful in the fight against slavery. But Garrison survived the challenge, and Torrey and the other rebels created a rival antislavery society and an overtly antislavery political party, the Liberty Party.

Still, Torrey needed a way to support his wife and two children, so he devised a new career: journalist, as Washington correspondent for small abolitionist newspapers in the north. He moved south at the end of 1841 and almost immediately stumbled upon a promising story—a slaveholders' convention in Maryland's capital, Annapolis. Ousted from the gathering, Torrey was surrounded by a hostile proslavery crowd and jailed for two days, mainly for his own protection. He wrote his adventure up for his client newspapers, and the local press covered it as well.

One of those intrigued by the news of this crazy young white man who had confronted the slaveholders and been jailed for his trouble was a Black shoemaker looking for partners in the fight against the slave system. It happened that Elizabeth Smallwood did the laundry for Torrey's Washington boardinghouse, and Thomas asked his wife to arrange an introduction. The shoemaker and the would-be journalist met across a chasm of race, class, age (Smallwood was forty, Torrey twenty-eight), formal education, and life experience. But they had one important thing in common: a blazing fury at slavery. Both men had spent years *talking* about slavery—Smallwood in the debates over colonization, Torrey in the battles over abolition strategy. Now they wanted to *act*. Together, they concocted a daring and ambitious scheme. They would organize escapes by the wagonload. By stripping the slaveholders of their valuable, unpaid workers, they hoped to undermine their morale and weaken support for the institution. If tens of thousands of dollars' worth of human property (in today's dollars) vanished overnight, what slaveholder would choose to stick with the system? Smallwood called it his "tax" on the system: "In any other form, such a tax would make a rebellion! I mean to tax them twice that, next year!"[10]

A clandestine operation like theirs is hard to document nearly two centuries later. But from Smallwood's later account in his memoir, from Torrey's occasional written references, and from a few independent sources, it is clear that they managed to build a network of allies and begin sending north wagonloads of ten, fifteen, or even twenty men, women, and children every two or three weeks.

Smallwood, who sometimes drove the wagon and sometimes recruited a driver, described the three-night journey to Pennsylvania, traveling only by dark. The first night the wagon would reach Baltimore, where Smallwood had recruited Jacob Gibbs, a Baltimore housepainter, to be his steadfast ally. Gibbs, called Mr. G. in Smallwood's memoir, would help hide the fugitives in the daytime at his house on East Street or those of friends, and then drive them north the next night to near the Susquehanna River, the broad natural barrier in northern Maryland. The third night they would cross the river, sometimes with the aid of a friendly boatman, and sometimes daring to cross the bridge to Port Deposit, Maryland, and continue into Pennsylvania, where Quaker helpers would lead the party on to the abolitionist hotbed of Philadelphia.

From there the freedom seekers seem to have traveled largely on public transportation when they had raised sufficient funds—train or steamship to New York City, steamship up the Hudson River to Albany, and on to Canada by canal boat. Smallwood always urged those he was assisting not to stop until they reached British soil in Canada, where slavery had been abolished in 1833. Though some abolitionists encouraged the formerly enslaved to remain in the northern United States and join the political battle against slavery, Smallwood thought that on American soil they would still be in danger from slave catchers. He was right. Police constables from Baltimore regularly traveled the 350 miles to Albany, for instance, to capture runaways and return them south to collect the substantial rewards offered by slaveholders.

After August 1842, Smallwood was operating in Washington on his own. Torrey had returned north to take a new job as editor of one of his client newspapers, *Tocsin of Liberty*, published in Albany. But by then the rollicking dispatches from Washington ridiculing the slaveholders whose unpaid workers had disappeared were becoming familiar to readers of that newspaper, whose name meant "liberty bell." *Tocsin* had begun publishing Smallwood's dispatches in June, appending the Dickensian pseudonym, Samivel Weller, Jr., often shortened to Sam Weller. Though an early dispatch prompted a public apology from the editor, apparently for a ribald reference to Senator Henry Clay, Smallwood's writing drew such acclaim that it was soon used in advertisements for the newspaper.

It's worth pausing briefly to consider the persuasive evidence that Smallwood wrote these pseudonymous letters. Smallwood later, in his memoir, stated that the Weller letters were "written by me"[11] and that he had chosen the pseudonym "to avoid detection." Their contents often reflected intimate familiarity with Washington and its inhabitants. Many of the dispatches suggest that their author had been personally involved in the escapes he was describing. It is possible that Charles Torrey advised or collaborated on the first three letters, written in the summer of 1842 when he was still in Washington. (The first letter begins with the abrupt address "Dear Goodwin," and Torrey probably knew the editor, Edwin W. Goodwin, better than Smallwood did.) It is also possible that Torrey brought his editor's pen to some dispatches published later, when he was the newspaper's editor. But there is every reason to trust Smallwood's claim of authorship, and neither Torrey nor anyone else ever made a competing claim. In 1844, after Smallwood was in Toronto, the "Samivel Weller" pseudonym was used for a few of Torrey's pieces for the Albany paper, where he was no longer editor. But those are clearly written by Torrey, and either he or an editor presumably decided to try to take advantage of the pseudonym Smallwood had made popular.

Smallwood's Sam Weller dispatches are sui generis, the work of a brilliant stylist driven by both his passion against slavery and his literary ambition. They can be challenging to read at first—they are allusive, archly ironic, and sometimes veer in tone from gleeful sarcasm to sober condemnation. (I have added brief summaries at the top of each dispatch to aid the reader.) But they are a remarkable journalistic, literary, and historical achievement, and one for which Smallwood has never received proper credit.

The dispatches turned the antebellum social world topsy-turvy, mounting a mocking assault on the ideologues of slavery who by the 1830s defended the institution as a kindness to captured Africans and their descendants. Countering the abolitionists, they argued that the African "savages" were incapable of looking after their own affairs, so the enlightened slaveholders were doing them a charitable service by supplying them with useful work, food, and lodging. Smallwood turned this on its head. In his Sam Weller dispatches, the slaveholders are the incapable ones—befuddled dimwits who are unable even to cook their own meals or drive their own carriages. "The stupidity of some slaveholders is very great,"[12] he declared, mocking them for advertising rewards for runaways who had long been safe in Canada. "A shrewd slave has wit enough at any time to get round a lazy, mole-eyed slaveholder,"[13] he wrote. "Even the Fullers," he added, referring to a family that had relocated from the north, "lost so much of their Yankee 'cuteness [acuteness] by becoming slaveholders, that HENSON disappeared from before their face and eyes in the middle of the afternoon, when three of them were watching him!"

One prominent proslavery voice in Smallwood's time was that of Thomas Roderick Dew, president of the College of William & Mary, who avowed that both slaveholders and the enslaved benefited from the bondage system. "Why, then, since the slave is happy, and happiness is the great object of all animated creation," Dew asked, "should we endeavor to disturb his contentment by infusing into his mind a vain and indefinite desire for liberty—a something which he cannot comprehend?"[14]

Dew's preposterous contention was at once provoking and inspirational for Smallwood. Smallwood and friends had helped on his way north one Joseph Chapman, who had fled his enslaver in Norfolk, Virginia. "Poor, benighted fellow! He had never read the convincing arguments of Rev. Mr. DEW,—(alas! he could not read!),"[15] Smallwood wrote. In other words, because Chapman had been prevented by the slave system from learning to read, he had not been able to read Dew's work to discover just how happy he should be! It was a characteristic jujitsu move by Smallwood, turning the slaveholders' claims against them and exposing their positions to the derisive laughter they richly deserved.

At the same time, Smallwood always insisted on asserting the full humanity of the enslaved. Sometimes he was jocular, as when he declared of the escaped Sophy Jackson that, "Sophy you know, left Washington a year ago, on the grand tour!"[16] Wealthy whites were able to go on the grand tour of European capitals? Well, the enslaved had their own version, with even greater rewards. A twenty-year-old man named Hanson "happens to think himself a man! and so he went to the Springs," Smallwood wrote, referring to Saratoga Springs in Upstate New York, "and sprung over to Canada!"[17]

At other moments, Smallwood's wrath competed with his wit. He was especially contemptuous of slaveholders' pretense that their enslaved workers had no family names, a privilege apparently reserved for whites. Slaveholders who offered rewards for runaways used a standard formula in their advertisements, as did an enslaver named George Gardiner, of Charles County, Maryland: "Henry, who calls himself Henry Edelen" had run away, he wrote, offering $50 for his return.

"Pray what should he 'call himself,' Mr. Gardiner?"[18] Smallwood asked. "It may be that your phrase is only part of that despicable system by which slaveholders are led to deny to their victims a *family name*, as if their family relations were not to be acknowledged even in words."

Smallwood exposed slaveholder after slaveholder—for raping an enslaved woman, for branding an enslaved man with a red-hot key, for killing another man with a "piece of old cart tire," for being repeatedly outsmarted by the captive workers who slipped away and never returned. His newspaper dispatches become a wide-ranging, eyewitness commentary on the state of slavery in his time and a persuasive answer to its defenders. He described the close relationship between the slaveholders and slave traders and the early police forces in Washington and Baltimore. He wrote of the domestic slave trade that was ripping families apart, "the Great National Slave Market" of the

Chesapeake, and the way the threat of sale to the deep south was motivating the enslaved to flee north. He wrote feelingly of the plight of free African Americans like himself, who lived under a despotism not experienced by their white neighbors, subject to nighttime curfews, travel restrictions, and myriad discriminatory rules. "You see that the constitution and laws of our country afford even the free man little protection against the tyranny of the slaveholders," Smallwood wrote.[19]

Smallwood kept operating, and writing, through most of 1843 with few pauses, and the literary quality and erudition displayed in his newspaper pieces may have been his best disguise: Few slaveholders would have suspected their author was a formerly enslaved shoemaker with no formal education. For months, Smallwood was able to turn the social invisibility of African Americans to powerful advantage, lurking among the slaveholders at the market or the train station and eavesdropping on their complaints about escapes. Frustrated slaveholders offered rewards in both Washington and Baltimore for the capture of whoever was responsible for the wave of escapes. But eventually the enslavers reading the newspaper columns lambasting them by name, and the police who served the slaveholders' interests, began to wonder about the shoemaker.

Smallwood got wind of the suspicions and curtailed his activities, turning over the clandestine nighttime drives to others. He concluded that Washington might soon be too dangerous for him and his family. By July 4, 1843, Smallwood was in Toronto on a brief reconnaissance trip—and prefiguring the famous later address of Frederick Douglass, "What to the Slave Is the Fourth of July?" Smallwood, relishing his time on Canadian soil, reflected that in the United States, "I would have been compelled painfully to witness as I had done for many years their hypocritical demonstrations in honour of a day, which they say, brought to them freedom; but I sorrowfully knew that it was in honour of a day that brought to me, and my race among them, the most degrading, tyrannical and soul-withering bondage that ever disgraced the world or a nation."[20]

By October, the Smallwoods—now with a fifth child—were safe in Toronto. But the next month, Thomas agreed to try to help free the wives and children of four men who had escaped to Toronto, three with Smallwood's help. He reunited with Torrey in Albany, and the men agreed to try to pull off one more mass escape from Washington, which had become dangerous territory. They managed to send off two of the wives to take their children north and join their husbands in Toronto—the other two "declined to come." Smallwood arranged to hide a wagon in the barn of a friend and was loading it with freedom seekers when the officers of Washington's Auxiliary Guard, a new police unit that Smallwood had pilloried in his Sam Weller dispatches, suddenly swooped in. Smallwood's detailed account of his escape on foot, his last meeting with Torrey in Baltimore, and his flight along the same path on which he had sent so many others would become the most exciting passage in his memoir.

Finally settled in Toronto for good, Smallwood started a new business: the manufacture and sharpening of saws, probably a response to the building boom then underway in the growing city. He became a notable figure in the small Black community, sometimes referred to as "The Rev. Thomas Smallwood" and active in church affairs and political life. He did not shy away from a fight and became embroiled in a debate over an all-Black church versus an integrated church (which Smallwood favored) and the direction of a Black community newspaper (Smallwood sued to recover his investment). His business thrived, and his children did well in school and in the workplace—though tragically, they would all predecease him.

New editors at the *Albany Weekly Patriot*, which had prospered from his Sam Weller letters, had rudely rejected a submission in a note to him published in the newspaper, so his writing came to a halt. But in 1851, stung by claims that he had profiteered off the escapes, he wrote and engaged a Toronto printer to publish a short memoir with a long name: *A Narrative of Thomas Smallwood, (Coloured Man:) Giving an Account of His Birth—The Period He Was Held in Slavery—His Release—and Removal to Canada, etc. Together with an Account of the Underground Railroad. Written by Himself.*

Smallwood's *Narrative*, his other major work after the Sam

Weller dispatches, is sometimes brilliant, sometimes frustrating. When it has been noticed by scholars it has generally been classified as a slave narrative, but Smallwood devotes only a few paragraphs to his life in slavery, moving quickly to his main subject, the escapes he had organized. What he calls his "simple narrative of unvarnished facts" is in fact packed with literary and historical allusions by this deeply self-educated man: He all but pummels the reader in the opening pages with Semiramis, Assyrians, Milton, Napoleon, Webster, Dr. Johnson, Young, Lord Brougham, Wordsworth, Curran, Cowper, Campbell, Byron, Longfellow, Burns, Shakespeare . . . And he includes a short biography of David Walker, whose 1829 essay denouncing slavery[21] and colonization had been an inspiration. The former shoemaker, proprietor of a saw factory, is staking his claim as a man of letters. Smallwood says his *Narrative* has a practical purpose—to counter the "slanders" to which he had been subjected. But it must have been an immense pleasure for him to once again be writing for the public, and there are some moments when he reprises the satirical voice of Sam Weller. He describes in detail one August 1842 wagonload of fifteen people he sent north (with Torrey in the driver's seat) and then relishes the chaos the disappearances must have set off among pampered slaveholders:

> Morning arrived, and with it a terrible uproar. One had no one to get breakfast, Ann had absconded taking with her all her children; another had no one to black the boots, to set the table, and to wait breakfast, Bill had taken French leave [i.e., skipped work], and gone about his business; and a third, had no one to drive the coach to church; others were also in as bad a fix.[22]

More often, though, Smallwood adopts a sober style, recounting his escape operation and its achievements and adding observations about the United States and its hypocrisy, the domestic slave trade, and life for a Black man in Canada.

He describes the most complex and dangerous phase of his clandestine procedure: the covert, late-night gathering of those heading north, who had to slip out of several households, cross the dangerous city, and avoid police enforcing a 10:00 p.m. curfew for Black people and the slave catchers trolling for reward money. Smallwood writes in his memoir that he advised them to walk alone, to draw less attention, to the always-changing spot in the "suburbs" of Washington where the wagon awaited. His detailed account of the three-night path to Pennsylvania, and the "places of deposit," or safe houses, along the way, is especially valuable. He describes the considerable costs involved, notably for renting or buying a wagon and a team of horses. He expends many words on aggrieved accounts of his betrayal by a few Black men whom he trusted, and who for cash turned over the freedom seekers in their care to slave traders.

His *Narrative* offers eyewitness accounts of the domestic slave traders who operated legally and openly in Washington and Baltimore, and many of those who gathered the courage to join an escape attempt did so because they feared they were about to be sold south, away from their families. He explains more fully his conviction that there would be no end to the vicious inequity white Americans and their laws imposed on African Americans, free as well as enslaved:

> It is true, the coloured people have as good a right to live in the United States, and enjoy the fat of the land, as their oppressors, but *"might overcomes right," where tyrants rule.* Did not our fathers fight side by side with their fathers, against the sires of the best friends they now have, to win that independence they now so much boast of? Yes they did! And the only reward they received is a refusal on their part to permit them to enjoy a share of the freedom they had so nobly helped them to gain, and to oppress their children down to the last turn of the screw.[23]

Smallwood was prescient, too, about what it would take to end the slave system, foreseeing the coming conflagration: "I believe the long suspended blow against that republic and the final emancipation of their victims are close at hand, and will be attended with a terrible and bloody breaking up of their present system."[24]

By the time the bloody breakup actually arrived, Smallwood was a solid citizen of Toronto, and he and his eldest son, also Thomas, were both members of a committee of Black Toronto residents chosen to write an "Address to the Colored Citizens of Canada"[25] on the progress of the Civil War in the United States. Their statement welcomed Lincoln's Emancipation Proclamation while noting that it was incomplete, urged Canadians to support the Union cause, and offered fervent good wishes: "We extend our sympathy to President Lincoln in the prosecution of the great work for freedom. We trust that the Union armies will be strengthened and sustained, and that they will go on 'conquering and to conquer,'" this last phrase from the book of Revelation.

Smallwood lived to eighty-two, a remarkable age for the time, but it must have been bittersweet: he was predeceased by his wife and all five of their children. Charles Torrey, as far as I can determine, never mentioned Smallwood in public writings or private correspondence. Smallwood went unmentioned in the 1847 biography of Torrey compiled by an ally after his death; nor was he mentioned in an 1849 remembrance of the Rev. Abel Brown, a key abolitionist ally in Albany on the route north. Having started a new life in Canada, Smallwood left no cadre of American or Canadian admirers of his heroic but clandestine work and his writings, and he and his work went virtually unmentioned in the century following his death in 1883. His newspaper dispatches—which, of course, did not bear his name—were scattered around the country in libraries that preserved a few copies of *Tocsin of Liberty* or *Albany Weekly Patriot*. His *Narrative*, printed at Smallwood's expense in modest numbers, was all but lost.

The *Narrative* was rediscovered in the 1980s by Henry Louis Gates, Jr.,[26] in *Figures in Black: Words, Signs, and the "Racial" Self*, where Gates called the *Narrative* "largely unknown" and quoted Smallwood's captivating recollection of the attention he got for learning to read, which Gates compared with a James Baldwin essay. In 2000, The Mercury Press published a new, paperback edition[27] of the *Narrative* with a useful introduction by Richard Almonte. The following year, the University of North Carolina made Smallwood's memoir available online in its invaluable project *Documenting the American South.* Also in 2001, Hilary Russell drew extensively on the *Narrative*[28] for her account of the underground railroad in Washington. Since then, several authors have discussed Smallwood in books about his era, most notably Stanley Harrold, who included a brilliant chapter on Smallwood and Charles Torrey in his 2003 book *Subversives: Antislavery Community in Washington, D.C., 1828–1865*. Among the scholars who have published on the *Narrative* in recent years, Sandrine Ferré-Rode wrote in 2013[29] about how Smallwood plays his story off the conventions of the slave narrative; Nele Sawallisch in 2018 published on Smallwood's radicalism[30] and his position in Black nineteenth-century Toronto; and most recently, Bryan Sinche, in his study of self-publication[31] in nineteenth-century African American literature, found the *Narrative* is "much more than the story of a single life, or of the Underground Railroad," amounting to a serious critique of the antislavery movement. The Cornell University Library has recently begun selling a paperback facsimile edition of the *Narrative*[32] without annotations.

If Smallwood's memoir was neglected by most scholars of slavery and antebellum America, his newspaper dispatches have been all but forgotten, occasionally cited for facts but never examined as literature. Stanley Harrold was perhaps the first scholar to examine and quote them, notably in his pathbreaking 2000 article "On the Borders of Slavery and Race: Charles T. Torrey and the Underground Railroad,"[33] and later in his book *Subversives*. E. Fuller Torrey, in his excellent 2013 biography[34] of his distant relative Charles Torrey, makes good use of a few of Smallwood's Weller pieces, as has Tom Calarco in his many works on the underground railroad.[35] Though his focus is on the *Narrative*, Sinche is the rare scholar to attempt a comprehensive reading of the dispatches, which he compares with the later work of Ida B. Wells on lynching.

This is a very modest body of scholarship, in which Smallwood is sometimes in the shadow of his young protégé, Torrey. In *Flee North*, I attempted for the first time to tell the full story of Smallwood, piecing together his biography, using newspaper databases to determine that he had named the underground railroad, and treating his newspaper dispatches as a unique literary work. But many gaps remain in Smallwood's life story. Who were his parents? Did he travel to New Hampshire and Connecticut, as his Sam Weller persona claims? How did Smallwood mail dispatch after dispatch to the Albany newspaper without raising suspicion at the post office? Could unpublished writings by this remarkable talent survive somewhere? Is there a photograph or other image of this man, who lived well into the photography era? Did he ever cross paths, after leaving Washington for Toronto, with Frederick Douglass or Harriet Tubman? What were his major literary influences, beyond David Walker and Charles Dickens? How do his writings fit into the canon of African American literature?

Thomas Smallwood, who cared deeply about how he and his achievements would be remembered, might be gratified at the recent surge of interest. He is an extraordinary figure in American life and letters, deserving of far greater public renown and scholarly study than he has received.

SCOTT SHANE

# A Note on the Text

Minor misprints and odd spellings that may be printer's errors have been corrected (for example, *abjoining* for *adjoining*; *ihence* for *hence*; *chattles* for *chattels*; *waggon* for *wagon*, *Torry* for *Torrey*, *Habertigrass* for *Havre de Grace*, *Gannet's Square* for *Kennett's Square*). I have preserved spellings that Smallwood altered for effect, usually to capture Sam Weller's Cockney dialect, such as *verry* and *wery* for *very*; likewise I have kept his unusual phonetic spelling of a racial slur as "neger" in two passages. Some archaic spellings are retained to convey a sense of the period, as well as British spellings reflecting Smallwood's residence in Toronto. In addition, Smallwood or his printer used few paragraph breaks, so many more have been added for easier reading.

# The Writings of Thomas Smallwood

# THE "SAM WELLER" LETTERS

# *TOCSIN OF LIBERTY*,

## June 28, 1842

*In the first of the "Sam Weller" letters, Smallwood establishes the custom of reprinting a slaveholder's runaway ad; asks the Albany editor to send a copy of the issue containing his letter to the named slaveholder, a request that would become standard; displays his taste for Charles Dickens, from whom he borrowed the pseudonym "Samivel Weller, Jr."; and refutes the enslaver's claim that Levi Carroll left "without the slightest provocation" by revealing she intended to sell Carroll south, away from his wife and child.*

$100 REWARD.

Ran away from the subscriber on Tuesday 14th inst., a negro man slave, who calls himself Levi Carroll, about 28 or 30 years of age; dark complexion, rather a pleasing countenance when in conversation, about 5 feet 7 inches high. He left home without the slightest provocation, where he has a wife and child. He has a mother living with a Mr. Brashcans, &c.

MARGARET A. CULVER,

JUNE 20TH. WASHINGTON CITY.

Dear Goodwin:—Please reprint from the National Intelligencer[1] of (Monday) the 20th, an advertisement for $100 reward for Levi Carroll, a fugitive slave from Washington, D.C. and send it to the *lady* who advertises him a copy of your paper, to assure her that she need give herself no further trouble respecting Mr. Carroll, as he is amply able to take care of himself, and especially, he deems it his duty "to beware of widows."[2] Perhaps Mrs. Culver has forgotten that she recently sold *one* of her slaves to the trader; and that Levi, though she may consider it "no provocation" to induce him to strive to gain his freedom, was well aware of her *benevolent* intention to sell him. Also, away from the society of his FREE WIFE AND CHILD.

Thank God! Mrs. Margaret A. Culver, your victim has escaped you; and you will not see him again till you meet him before God's throne of judgment, when HE will demand of you an account of your conduct in withholding the hire of the laborers, and selling your fellow-men, in the shackles. For shame! Are you a woman? Have you a human heart? Then let go your hold upon the other victims of lawless power whom you retain in wicked bondage! Are not some of them kind hearted, affectionate women? Will you crush your *own sisters* under the yoke? Where is that humanity, that gentleness of heart, that warmth of affection which were the love of your deceased husband; will you not show these qualities in dealing with your dependents? Depend upon it, you will never get Levi back again. If you have $100 to spare which you offer for his apprehension, and will be humane enough to use it for *his welfare*, instead of your own selfish ends, please enclose a draft on New-York, for that amount to the EDITOR OF THE TOCSIN, and, though he never *saw* your friend Carroll, and knows not where he is, a kind friend of his *does* know, and will convey the money safe to Mr. Carroll's address. Do send the $100! Why, Levi may need it to set him up in business; and, as you have heretofore, had *all his earnings*, you may afford so small a sum to aid him in setting up shop on his own hook! If you don't, I shall advise him to "keep dark, and never show that countenance which you well say is pleasing in conversation," where your negro widows can get him. In short, my advice to him will be in the language of Boz:[3]

"Beware of widdies! Cause they're wery deceitful."

I would only add, that you might do well by applying the $100 to helping Levi's wife and child on towards Canada; or at least to Harrisburg or Pittsburgh, where he can send somebody for them. And as they are free, you would prove that a "widdie" may have a *tender heart*, after all.

Yours truly,

SAM WELLER.

# *TOCSIN OF LIBERTY,*

## July 27, 1842

*Smallwood has a fine time roasting a D.C. slaveholder whom he dubs a "soft headed man-thief" and makes clear that the escaped Horace Wilson is safe in Canada. He advises the slaveholder to send the reward money north to assist his former unpaid worker to get a new start. Addressing early speculation about his identity, "Sam Weller" insists he is not part of the Albany Vigilance Committee—the antislavery group in that city—and taunts the slaveholders about their inability to identify him.*

### Property Become Men.

FIFTY DOLLARS REWARD.—Ran away from the undersigned, on Monday night, the 11th inst. my negro man HORACE WILSON. He is about 34 years of age, 5 feet 10 or 11 inches high; is of a dark color, very erect and quick motioned, affable manners and tolerably fluent tongue; dress not known, as he had a variety. I think it likely he has fraudulently obtained papers. I will give $20 if said runaway be taken in the District of Columbia, $30 if taken in any adjoining State, and $50 if apprehended elsewhere, and secured so that I recover him again.

FRANCIS HAYRE.

Can't do it, no how, Mr. Hayre; you meant to have a lad work altogether too cheap. Horace Wilson is a noble fellow, worth $650 at least, in your man-market; and without *my* help, your chance of getting your man trap upon his now free limbs, is not worth half a straw! I will give you a *little* information *gratis*. Horace has "papers," not obtained "fraudulently" however, but very cordially given to him by the "General Forwarding Co."[1] which is engaged in extensive business, in the *transformation of chattels into men*, with a large *cash* capital of *willing hands* and *willing hearts*. In behalf of said company, I had the pleasure of giving him a *free pass, or letter of credit*. His papers are *good*, and have long since taken him beyond the reach of your blood hounds.

$20 only, if caught in this district; it ought to be $50 at least. If you will send that sum to me, at New York, I will tell you a secret, to wit, that he didn't *stop long* in your petty 10 miles square. Nor will your $30 catch him in a neighboring State. Why you soft headed man-thief, that sum would have given him a quick passage to Ohio, or Boston, or Charlestown and hence to Jamaica, by water. I'll tell you what; in consideration of Horace's verry good qualities, and your *tender regard* for him, which has led *to lay up all his wife's earnings*, so carefully that he got scarcely enough to go off with; and out of pity for your loss, if you will *come down literally*, and send me $250 to Portland, Maine, I will tell you exactly where he will be on the 1st of August, 1842. I may as well do it now, on second thoughts. So here it is. He will be making a real *Washingtonian experience speech*, in a meeting called to celebrate West India Emancipation, somewhere 750 miles from his kind master. But I am much afraid that you have to *capture Bermuda*, push Quebec into a cocked hat, and put a Paischan shot[2] through Halifax and Jamaica, before you can get him back. Besides, as he has a *free wife*, it will be an act of kindness if you, my dear fellow, will just hand me over *that* $50 to help her go on after him for though you took such a fancy to his earnings: It can't be supposed that you wish to delay the happy hour of his reunion with his dear wife; *especially* as you cannot help it, do what you will!

In conclusion, I advise you to call on Mrs. Culver, somewhere near the City Hall, and talk over your Montreal losses! It will be a good deed in you to "visit the widow" in her affliction, especially as she is *rather* pretty, and there is no *Hayre* on her upper lip! Go comfort the widdy, and she will comfort you!

Your friend,

SAM WELLER.

P. S. Samivel Weller wishes to say to the Friend of Man, and all that sort of people, that he is *not* a member of the Albany Vigilance Committee, and don't live any where near that place. In fact, he lives in *no* particular spot; but where humanity has work to do, and the pay is *small*, he hopes to be found doing his small share of it.

N. B. I just learned that two other gentlemen from the city of Washington, left there about the same time with Horace Wilson.

☛ And this is to give notice to the old constable *and professional man catcher*, the *brother* of the mistress of ROBERT, that it will be of no sort of use for him to spend *that* $1,000, for he won't find him. Nor will the *lame brother* of the owner of *Levi S.* be able to catch up with a fine active lad who has *two good legs* of his own. I wish that Robert and Levi, however, would remember not to stop at *Richmond*, or any other place between this and New Orleans; and meanwhile to keep a bright lookout for these old f(r)iends!

Will the N. A. Standard, and Demosthenian Shield,[3] please notice this N. B., to give the alarm that these man hyenas are on the track.

Yours, SAM.

# *TOCSIN OF LIBERTY,*

## August 10, 1842

*In this letter, the first recorded use of "underground railroad" in print, Smallwood reprints three runaway ads from the Washington, D.C., newspapers and dissects them, displaying his inside knowledge of the people who fled and their frustrated enslavers, including "widders" (widows). To lampoon slaveholders and police, he introduces the absurd notion that people must be escaping by "'under ground rail-road' or 'steam balloon,'" since the befuddled former owners cannot otherwise explain these overnight disappearances.*

### Business in Washington, D.C.

RAN AWAY from the subscriber, residing on East Capitol street, Washington city, on the night of Monday, the 11th instant, my servant man ROBERT BARNS, aged about twenty-five years, 5 feet 9 inches high, and rather stout, large eyes, with a scar above one of them, fine teeth, ears bored, bushy head, and of a swarthy copper color, with an open, pleasant countenance. He had on when he left home, a blue cloth coat with velvet collar, and gilt buttons, nearly new, black vest, and cravat, light drilling pantaloons and boots, and took with him other summer clothing, and a silver watch. He went off in company with three other negro men, one of whom has since been taken.

When apprehended and brought home I will pay the following reward for him: If taken in the District of Columbia, or either of the adjoining counties, $30; if taken in any other part of Maryland, $50; and if taken beyond the limits of that State, $100.

A. M. HARRINGTON.

The subscriber is extremely sorry for *Miss* A. M. Harrington's loss. Mr. Barns *has* "an open pleasant countenance," is a fine manly fellow, and you ought not to have served him so! Woman! I charge you before your maker, with *robbing* that young man! aye, of keeping him in ignorance, so that he could not read the word of God.

You even demanded of him an account of his *presents*, and generally took them from him! Why you're worse than that *widder* I told about some time ago, though she was a shark sure enough, and the way she *did* swear when she found Mr. Carroll was missing, was a caution to the 4th commandment. Verry sorry a lady has no more government over her tongue! sorry to contradict a lady but can't help it. Your friend *did not* leave in that company, and *not one* of his company has been taken, or ever will be. And news from the district shows that Mr. Fuller's man, who *was* taken up at Williamsport, departed to *parts unknown* three days after, and has not since been heard of by his tyrant. By the way, Mr. Azariah Fuller stands a smart chance of hearing some *black facts* about his history told, that won't read quite so well among his New England acquaintances!

Here's another fact.

$100 REWARD—Ran away from the subscriber, living in Washington county, D. C., on the 18th ultimo,[1] a negro man named HENRY HAWKINS, about twenty-seven or twenty-eight years of age, supposed to be five feet eight or ten inches high, rather inclined to be copper-colored, broad forehead, thin visage and front teeth very much decayed. Had on when he left a pair of coarse, brown linen pantaloons, a light mixed cloth round jacket, a new cotton shirt, and an old fur hat, and took with him a carpet bag containing a dark frock coat, a pair of drab pantaloons, and a pair of fine boots. When spoken to he has a pleasant countenance. I will give for the above described slave $50 if taken in the District of Columbia and $100 if taken in any of the States, and secured in jail so that I get him again.

He formerly belonged to Mr. Alexander Talburt living on 7th street, has a free wife on the corner of 10th and H streets, Washington, and a mother at the Navy Yard by the name of Sarah Brown.

THOS. A. SCOTT

Pretty accurate description Mr. Scott! only not quite exact as to the clothing.—Poor fellow, he *couldn't* take all the clothing you speak of, from his haste! I half suspect you describe so much clothing merely to give northern people the idea that you *clothed him well*, when *you know* that he had to buy for himself, and that it was *your cruelty* to him, that made him disappear by that same "under ground rail-road" or "steam balloon," about which one of your city constables was swearing so bitterly a few weeks ago when complaining, that the "d——d rascals" got off so, and that *no trace* of them could be found! Very true!

Mr. Scott! Will you inform the editor of the Tocsin, how *Mr. Hawkins*' mother should be called Sarah *Brown*, with no second marriage. I know you are too good a man to allow that "amalgamation" or any *sich* thing,[2] takes place in your city. Take care sir! It is true his boots are "fine," but I am quite sure *you* didn't buy them for him, and you are quite mistaken about the "carpet bag." He could get it to the depot of the subterranean rail-road, without notice. By the way! Just to show you how great *fools* your constables are, I will add for your *instruction and consolation*, that Mr. Hawkins was one evening, some time after he fled, in *Dr. Hall's room* in the *medical college*, standing behind the door, when the puppies wanted to come in, but couldn't 'cause the "Doctor didn't allow folks to come into his room when he wasn't there." Narrow escape, wasn't it! The way Henry laughed when he told it, showed his *want of teeth* about which your advertisement speaks, and for which such a *humane* man as you ought to be able to account in a man so young, or you will be grievously suspected of knocking them out.

> $5 REWARD—Ran away on the night of the 22nd inst., from the residence of the subscriber, corner of 11th and L streets, Washington, D.C., negro boy Henry (commonly called Henry Clay). He is about ten years of age, is a light copper color, and has tolerably straight black hair. Had on when he left a pair of dark cloth pantaloons, light striped roundabout and a straw hat. When last heard of he was on board of one of the long boats employed in bringing wood from Dumfries and other places in Virginia to this city; the name of the boat was supposed to be Henry Clay. The above reward will be given upon his being delivered to me, free of cost, at the place above mentioned.
>
> MARTHA D. ALLEN

Mrs. Allen! Mrs. Martha D. Allen, corner of 11th and L streets, I'm ashamed of you! "HENRY CLAY" run off, and you only offer five dollars for him! Oh! I see; it is the young one![3] Allow me to note a few points in your very entertaining advertisement.

1. "Negro." Why you say he is of "a light copper color"! Had you said "nearly white, long face, high narrow forehead," it would have suited quite as well.

2. Will you tell us *why* he is "commonly called Henry Clay," of all the Henry's in the world? Is it from the general understanding about his FRATERNITY?

How does the idea correspond with the "tolerably straight black hair," and the other features of resemblance to his namesake! Why, exactly! But remember madam, I advise you to drop *no hints* on this subject, as it might hurt Mr. Clay's political prospects, and wound the feelings of his "whig *abolition*" friends, if you are not very careful what you say. For consider, my sweet woman, that it is now, *in fact*, seven or eight years since Mr. Clay sowed his wild oats, and can't *you suppose*, (merely *suppose*,) that it is ten or eleven, and that this was the *last wild oats he sowed*? I beseech you, be prudent! One thing more.

I am very much afraid you won't see young master Clay again. Nay, I fear you will be thought *miserly*, and in fact, *no good whig*, for offering only a paltry five dollars for one who bears such an honored name, and who has so good a right to bear it too! Mrs. Allen! Mrs. Allen, sweet Martha, (you used to be sweet when you was 20 years younger,) think what evil construction may, nay must, be put upon your conduct!

One word to your northern readers—Please Mr. Editor to suggest to them the propriety of raising a fund to defray the cost of *advertising* fugitives. It costs so much, and so little is got by it, that the poor poverty stricken slave-holders are getting unable to bear it. *Perhaps* it is on that account, and *perhaps* it is to *throw some fugitives off their guard*, that several owners recently have refrained from advertising their missing property.

By the way, your printers, Mr. Editor, made as many queer blunders in printing my last piece, as Mr. Boz Dickens did in printing my, and my father's memoirs.—One who didn't know us might think we want up to speakin and writin good English, or American either. So pray tell 'em to be careful, and do send the three advertisers a copy of your paper, containing this piece of mine, and enclose your bills for printing to their address in Washington, for all these "business advertisements" come from the National Intelligencer.

Yours and Mrs. Allen's
Very humble servant,
SAM WELLER.

*All along shore, Liberty day Aug. 1 '42.*[4]

# *TOCSIN OF LIBERTY*,

## August 24, 1842

*Here Smallwood uses six more runaway ads to scold and ridicule the enslavers: their refusal to recognize the last names of the people they enslave; the biracial children they have fathered; their brutal exploitation of "two legged property." He shows off his erudition (Ovid's* Metamorphoses*) and his inside knowledge of Washington (Mrs. Sprigg's abolitionist boarders) and gleefully declares his recently christened underground railroad a state secret.*

### Runaway Property.

Mr. Tocsin,—

My information from the capital warrants me in saying, that my comments on the *two legged property converted into humanity*, greatly disturb those gentle loving spirits, ycleped slave holders. Somehow, these modern metamorphoses, more strange than any that Ovid ever knew or sung, become more and more frequent every day. I cut from a single number of the National Intelligencer, (which is the slave trader's and man-hunters' principal advertising sheet in that region,) a whole column of notices of walking property walked off! I subjoin a portion of them with appropriate comments.

> "$100 REWARD.—Ran away from the subscriber's residence, near Upper Marlboro, Prince George's county, Maryland, about the 20th of April last, my negro woman MATILDA, aged about 35 years; about 5 feet 1 or 2 inches high, generally called by the servants MATILDA BOWIE; a likely mulatto, with a very bushy head, which she keeps tied up with a handkerchief, and has a scar behind one of her

ears, occasioned by a bile. Her clothing cannot be described, as she had a variety.

"I will give $50 reward if taken in this State or District of Columbia, or $100 if taken out of the State or District, and delivered to me.

W. BOWIE BROOKE."

"The servants" are correct! A lady in Washington assured my informant that this "mulatto" girl has a *good right* to the name of Bowie; and so have *some of her children*, unless they *prefer* that of Brooke. The lady referred to, declared that she was rejoiced at Matilda's escape, for she had been very *brutally* used by her owner.

The stupidity of some slaveholders is very great. They advertise people a month after they are missing, when 24 hours is ample time for a shrewd slave to escape. For example, Mr. George H. Gardiner of Pleasant Hill P.O. Charles co. Md. advertises his dear friend and servant, "Henry, who calls himself Henry Edelen," as having run away on the 7th of July, in the Intelligencer for July 27.

The "yellow fellow," as Mr. G. calls him, is doubtless out of harm's way, long ago. Pray what should he "call himself," Mr. Gardiner? Do you mean to insinuate that his proper name is Henry GARDINER. Mark it! *I* don't mean to insinuate any such thing; Not I! It may be that your phrase is only a part of that despicable system by which slaveholders are led to deny to their victims a *family name*, as if their family relations were not to be acknowledged even in words. Mr. Gardiner, I'm *afeard* your $50 will hardly make Henry Edelen into plain Henry again.—The same general marks of folly appertain to the advertisement of the "*negro* boy Hensen," who is of a "*light copper color*," by Mr. Wm. T. Berry of Upper Marlborough, Prince George's co. Md. Ran away May 19th, advertised June 28th.—*Hope* the $100 offered, and the "*light* copper color," are not indications of paternal feelings in the advertiser! Ungrateful child, to leave his dear papa!

So too, Mr. G. Combs of Washington, D.C. is too late in advertising. Austin probably thought that a man 54 or 5 years old, was old enough to visit his wife without asking leave any longer. A man of that age, "a little bent" from hard service, is hardly worth your $40; so that your kind feelings towards an aged servant, Mr. G. Combs, must account for your care of him.

> "$100 REWARD.—On the 5th instant, my servant JACOB, a slave for life, left home with the avowed intention of going to Loudoun county, Virginia, to harvest.—I gave him a pass for that purpose. I now have reason to believe that he has made off, perhaps to Pennsylvania. He is very tall, from three to four inches above six feet high; not heavy built, but good size, and very active in his movements; black; very pleasant countenance when spoken to, regular features and good teeth. I do not recollect any particular marks about him. Is about 22 or 23 years of age, very intelligent, and a good deal of cunning. It is useless to describe his clothing, as he has no doubt procured new clothes, having without doubt a good supply of money.—He may have forged free papers, or procured the free papers of some of his free acquaintances.
>
> "I will give $50 for his apprehension in the State of Maryland, or $100 if taken in Pennsylvania, so that I may get him again."
>
> JOHN HARRY.
>
> "GEORGETOWN, D.C."
>
> "P. S. I wish to hire by the year, a servant to supply the place of the above. J.H."

Well, John Harry, I must say your P.S. shows your good sense; you have more than your neighbors give you credit for! I hope you will hire a *free* man. You have your *soft spot*, or you would not have trusted to the "avowed intention" of a shrewd fellow like Jake, who knew the way to the "underground rail-road."—Sorry I can't give you more information about him.

Out of sympathy with dear "Brother Lee," I add the following, as his *sister Martha* is willing that he should know that she is well, and "hopes these few lines will find him in the enjoyment of the same blessins." A friend of mine happened to be in Baltimore the night your handsome sister left. She *scorns* the word "absconded." No such thing! She went openly in the public vehicle as a member of your very respectable family ought to go. So take back your shabby word about one so *dear* to you, and so popular, as the following description shows.

> "$100 REWARD.—Ran away from the residence of the subscriber, during his absence from the city, a light mulatto slave woman, named MARTHA, aged about 26 years. She is above the ordinary size and inclined rather to be tall; has black eyes, and straight black hair. When spoken to appears to be indifferent and moody in her manner of replying; is quite likely, and had a large circle of acquaintances among her own color. [Which color is that Mr. Lee?—Ed. Tocsin.] She was seen here on Monday afternoon last, and must have absconded on that night or the following morning. She carried a variety of clothing, and was much addicted to dress and company.
>
> "She has no doubt made for the north or Pennsylvania, with some free or runaway negro fellow. Her mother and family reside in Washington, and she sometimes calls herself MARTHA LEE, *having been raised in the family*.[*!!*] The above reward will be given for her apprehension and delivery in Baltimore.
>
> Z. COLLINS LEE."

Subjoined are advertisements of *four* persons who seem to have left Washington the same night.

A friend informs me that *eight* left together in one way: and several more left by a vessel for Boston, about the same time!

> "$100 REWARD.—Ran away on the night of the sixth of this month, my slave man, by name ISAAC DORSEY, aged about 28 years. The said slave has an indelible mark on the

left side of the head, on or about the temple, caused by a burn; his ears are pierced for ear-rings. He is about five feet nine or ten inches high; his clothing cannot be described; he is civil when spoken to. The above slave has a father living in Montgomery county. He is also well acquainted in Fredericktown and county.

"At the same time a slave named JOSEPH LEE, the property of Mr. Griffith Coombe, about 22 years of age, 5 feet 8 or 10 inches high, neither stout nor thin.—He was dressed in a blue frock coat, and linen pantaloons; is accustomed to the care of horses; is civil when spoken to. The last named slave has probably accompanied the first. And the above reward will be given if they are brought to Washington city and lodged in jail; that is, if they are taken out of the District of Columbia or Montgomery county; if taken in Frederick, all of the above reward, and if nearer in proportion.

JAMES G. COOMBE."

These Messrs. Coombe are northern men, with robber, alias southern principles. The son, James G. is a physician. I should just like to ask him *if* he didn't feel *particularly* sheepish when *he met Dr. May* south east of the capitol a few days ago, when his contemptible trick of using a poor woman as an instrument (an unconscious one,) to find out how Dorsey and Lee escaped, failed of success?

I hope he won't take any offence at my bluntness! I would just hint to him, by way of caution, that the secret of the "underground rail-road," has never been communicated to any but the PRESIDENT and his CABINET: so that a few constables and an ignorant woman who knew nothing about it, won't help him very much!

I am very sorry to add that Mr. Shaw is *mistaken* as to David's clothing. Moreover, he is respectfully informed that *Liberty* has had the wonderful effect of *curing* David's impediment in his speech!—Mr. Shaw will find it hard even to recognize his voice again. And if Mr. THOMAS TALBURT does not wish to have a full length portrait of himself, drawn in *nature's* own dark colors, he had better send the Editor of the Tocsin some money for Woodland, instead of trying to get him back again!

> "$50 REWARD.—Ran away, on Saturday evening, the 6th instant,[1] from the subscriber, living near the Navy Yard, Washington, my negro man who calls himself JAMES WOODLAND. Said Woodland is about 35 years of age, of a copper color, about five feet ten inches high, good countenance and speaks free; has a scar on one side of his nose, and a scar on his forehead near the hair; a lump on the back of his neck, supposed to be occasioned by a sprain, as he has been employed in the Navy yard. He had on a black fur hat, linen roundabout, white shirt, and gray pantaloons. He took with him a new grass linen roundabout, a blue frock coat, and a pair of boots. It is believed that he has a free pass, and is making his way to a free state.
>
> "I will give twenty-five dollars if taken in the District or State of Maryland, and the above reward if taken in any other State, and secured so that I get him again.
>
> THOMAS TALBURT."

> "$100 REWARD.—Ran away from the subscriber, on Saturday night last, the 6th instant, residing in the outside on the farm called Brentwood, owned by Mrs. C. Pierson, about two miles north of the Capitol, a negro man named DAVID HAMILTON, about 21 years of age, six feet high, rather dark complexion, has a down look, and stammers when spoken to, and a large scar over the left eye, from a scald when young, which is very conspicuous. When he left had on coarse linen pants and cloth coat. I will give the above reward if taken over forty miles from the District; if within forty miles of the District, I will give fifty dollars; and if within the District fifteen dollars—if secured in some way that I can get him.
>
> JAMES A. SHAW."

[We cannot tell but some of the above chattels of the "peculiar institution" were among those of the "grand shipment of humanity," a few days ago, made up of *eighteen bales*, labelled by their own Creator, and destined to the free north beyond Ontario. We hope Sam will notify the proprietor of the Washington Hotel, Washington, D.C., that Henson Hutt was well when we saw him last, and that he may expect to hear from him in a few days from her Majesty's dominions. He is a fine smart young man. Henry Jefferson, from Washington, wished me to say to his master, he was well and thought he could take care of himself.—Ed. Tocsin.]

My news from Washington warrants me in laughing at Mr. Azariah Fuller and his sons a little. The great blockheads cannot yet account for the mysterious disappearance of their man! Let me explain it to you, sweet sirs! When you sent him down the avenue on that errand, it is true, you thought you watched him very close; but there were many people in the street at the time, and, though he was in his shirt sleeves, your eyes might fail to fix on him, just at the particular moment when he slipped into the door of the apothecary's shop on the corner of 11th street, and out of the other, that opens on the back street! How he went to another city and then sent for money to help him on, and escaped to Canada, it don't just now suit my purposes to tell you.

☛ But, allow me to assure you, that no abolitionist who is or has been in Washington, helped him off. And if I hear of any more complaints of your son and a constable making impertinent visits and inquiries about Mr. Leavitt and others, at Mrs. Sprigg's,[2] on Capitol Hill, I will make your name *stink* in New England as it does in Washington, for a slave-trader!—So please be careful! So no more at present from your faithful friend,

SAM WELLER.

*late of England.*
(See my life and dad's by Boz)

# *TOCSIN OF LIBERTY,*

## August 24, 1842

*Following an apology to the readers by the editor of* Tocsin of Liberty *for "objectionable" material in his previous dispatches, Smallwood defends himself, saying he was trying to be humorous and to lambaste the slaveholders and slave hunters. He cites the rambunctious style of Dickens's* Pickwick Papers *in his own defense. Neither the editor nor Smallwood specify what exactly caused offense, but a likely suspect was his joking in the August 10 edition about Senator Henry Clay possibly having fathered a boy by one of the women he enslaved.*

### "Sam Weller."

Mr. Tocsin:—Your correspondent begs pardon[1] of the very few *judicious* persons among your readers, who were offended by his style, which, for a *peculiar and valuable purpose*, was assumed rather in keeping with the character of "Sam Weller," than of the writer's own taste. The end in view, aside from exciting the smiles of the reader, (no sin I hope!) was to expose to contempt the slave hunters and advertisers of slave property. That the end has been reached, the *fluttering of the wounded clearly shows*, as your readers will learn, in a week or two. I am far from wishing to defend the *discretion* of every phrase I made use of. I have only to say, that *discretion and propriety* are not the leading traits of the characters of my father and myself, as delineated by our biographer, Mr. BOZ DICKENS!

Your readers will please notice, also, that the *most indiscreet* things in my *last article*, are some *incidental developments* of the every day life of slavery in Washington, that were furnished me by a *sure friend* in that city.

Your humble servant,

SAMUEL WELLER, Jr.

# *TOCSIN OF LIBERTY*,

## September 7, 1842

*Smallwood again refers to the newspaper's apology for his brazen earlier columns, and he pauses to note the paradox of making "fun" out of the dark deeds of slaveholders, who—in a turnabout—are "writhing" under his "lash." He pretends outrage that someone has mixed him up with the "obscure abolitionist" Charles Torrey. He scoffs at the business proposition of a Mississippi planter seeking to purchase an enslaved workforce with an ad in Washington.*

### Business at the Capital.

"TWO HUNDRED NEGROES WANTED.—The subscriber has a plantation, with a sufficiency of land attached, (in the most compact form, viz: embraced in a point between two streams) for 200 or 250 hands. The land is equal in quality of soil, timber and water, and secure against overflow, to any alluvial lands in the state, convenient to the Mississippi river, and contains extensive improvements, such as Grist Mill, Saw Mill, and Gin: a large quantity of land cleared and partially cleared, so that by the second year two thousand bales of four hundred pounds each can be made, if it be a good crop year, and more than a thousand the first year. I will enter into bond for the deficiency. There are near 400 acres of the tract, a very small—a very unusually small portion of which is not tillable.

My object is to form a copartnership with some one or two gentlemen, who will furnish the above number of hands, and I own one-third and they two-thirds; or a small number, and I own half. I have lived near seven years upon the place.—It has the best well of water I have seen, and is as healthy as any of the alluvial lands of the state. It is supposed to lay in the very centre of the cotton region on the Louisiana side of the Mississippi, 40 miles north of Natchez. The mortality among the black adults in the neighborhood, I think, for the last six years, has not exceeded one or two percent, per annum. Communications directed to me at New Carthage, Louisiana, will be attended to.

J. BUTLER."

Albeit, I come not from a *judicious* county, (my father and I being both of us, as Mr. Boz Dickens has shown, rather rough and homespun characters.) I even I, Samivel Weller, junior, will endeavor to comment on sundry matters in the newspapers, in a *werry* modest and sensible way,[1] for the *benefit of those* who are concerned!

☛ Let the judicious readers, (I grant they are so,) who took offence at my levities, please to remark one thing, viz: that I *had a purpose* in those articles, beyond the mere *fun* of it: the "fun" of commenting on atrocities at which the Pit might well blush!—"fun" indeed!

☛ Nevertheless, a sure and tried friend in Washington, declares that the end is already, in some measure answered. The slaveholders are writhing under the affliction of the lash! Some are *ashamed* to continue to advertise: some avoid it altogether. The Mr. Azariah Fuller alluded to in a former paper, has put himself to considerable trouble to interfere with the comfort of one of my *old and intimate friends*, the Rev. C.T. Torrey,[2] threatening him with beating, a mob, and sundry other minor evils, because he mistook Mr. Torrey for me, even me, Sam Weller, jr! The ignorant blunderhead! Is not *my* name carried to the world's end? Am I to be confounded with an obscure abolitionist, and *he* to be persecuted for my misdeeds! Mr. Torrey will probably tell his own story. It will be a rich "*devilopement*" as Mrs. Child says,[3] of the character of a "northern man with southern principles," in the small way.—Meanwhile, lest Mr. Torrey should be troubled again by these hyenas on my account, I beg you to assure them, that he and Samivel Weller, jr. are very, *very* different persons in their habits, views, feelings, characters, homes, names, looks, and every thing else! And farther, that while Mr. Torrey will, as heretofore, be occupied with more important matters, I, Samivel Weller, jr. will continue to SCOFF at, *annoy*, and *expose* the slaveholders, and their crooked ways, to their perfect mystification and great pain, during weeks and months to come! The ignoramuses! to think to catch *such* a weasel as I, asleep.

But it is time to turn to my first picture of the "peculiar institution," so very peculiar that it can't bear to be spoken of, much less laughed at.

Queer fellow, this Mr. Butler! In the city of WASHINGTON, the Nation's capital, he issues his *piratical* proposition, to any other wholesale plunderer of his species, to join with him in depriving 200 human beings of all their earnings on *shares*.

The mortality of "adult" negroes is only "one or two per cent. per annum"! Indeed! Fine healthy country that! Let us calculate the profits of the investment a little!

OUTLAY—200 negroes at $500, $100,000; as the tools are on hand, and the land ready; we will add nothing to the expenses for these items.

Interest on the amount so invested, (say $20,000,) at 6 per cent, $1,200 a year.—Interest on the purchasing of negroes, at 6 per cent, $6,000 a year. Loss by death 2 per cent, $2,000 a year. Food and other supplies for the plantation, at $20 a head for negroes, $4,000 a year: do. for three white families, (including the overseer's) at $2,000 each, $6,000.

Now count it up.

| | |
|---|---:|
| Interest on land, | $1,200 |
| Interest on "negroes," | 6,000 |
| DEATH, | 2,000 |
| Supplies, | 4,000 |
| Families, | 6,000 |
| | $19,200 |

So much, therefore, is to be wrung out of these poor children of sorrow, before any profit accrues from his investment.—Look at the

INCOME.—Crop 1,000 bales 1st year, 400 pounds each, short staple cotton, at an average price of 8 cents, comes to $32,000. Deduct for waste, expense of getting to market, and exchange, or cost of getting returns in *kind* as the plantation may require, say 1 cent a pound, equal to $4,000. This leaves the clear income at $28,000, and the clear profit on the investment at $9,000. This is a very little more than 7 1/2 per cent interest on the mere capital invested—not a very good promise to speculators. If I had made all the deductions truth would warrant from the profit, and all the just additions to the expenses, the clear income would turn out to be considerably *less* than 6 per cent, to say nothing of extraordinary casualties, failures of crops, fluctuations of prices, *runaway chattels* turning into MEN, (not uncommon even in Mississippi!) and other things that cannot be very well estimated. I'm afraid Johnny Butler won't have many offers!

N. B. He says nothing of the mortality among *children*, or the prevention of "breeding," and other evils by over-work, nor of the gradual wear and tear "of the adults."

> "$100 REWARD.—Ran away from the subscriber, on Sunday night, the 24th instant, a negro man named PETER MATTHEWS. He is about 27 years of age and about 5 feet 10 inches high, of a mulatto color, of good form, and generally very well looking; polite when spoken to, and speaks in a low tone of voice; hair black, and when he left bushy on the sides of his head. Peter is a good dining room servant, and carriage driver, in which capacity he has for the last five years been employed. He chews tobacco, and his teeth are not very good.
>
> He took with him a good assortment of clothing; such as recollected, are as follows: A green frock cloth coat, yellow buttons; a black cloth coat; gambroon and other pantaloons, light colored; and light colored vests, &c. with a black hat; fur cap (brown.)

I will give fifty dollars if the above negro be taken in the State of Maryland, and confined so that I will get him again, or one hundred dollars if taken in any other state, so that I can get him again; and thirty dollars if taken within the District of Columbia.

JAMES LARNED,

WASHINGTON, D.C."

Peter, the graceless scoundrel! when his loving master got him back a few weeks ago, and *went to such an expense about him*, wouldn't stay at home, after all! So one day he passed to Canada by the "under-ground rail-road." The way Mr. James Larned *did* swear when he went into the Bank of Washington to get the $100 to pay for catching him, fully proved his need of better instruction in the ten commandments! Peter was caught only four miles from the Pennsylvania line! He won't be caught again so easily!

Bad habit, that of chewing tobacco! I hope now that Peter is out of your grasp, Mr. Clerk,[4] he will reform in that particular. You should have saved your $100 for Peter's use, after he got to Canada!

☛ RETRIBUTION. Among the slaves recently escaped from Washington city to Canada, is a fine "boy," belonging to the man who *went down to Annapolis last winter, to stir up the mob against the Rev. C. T. TORREY.*[5] Eh, mister? I reckon you had better stay at home, and mind your own business, the next time; and perhaps you will have less to answer for, and suffer less in your pockets, too!

I will close by an item of *law*. The sale, I believe, did not take place, the debt being paid. But it shows how things *might* be done!

MARSHALL'S SALE.—In virtue of a writ of fieri facias[6] issued from the Clerk's Office of the Circuit Court of the District of Columbia for the county of Washington and to me directed, I expose at public sale, for cash on the 11th day of this month, at 11 o'clock, A.M. before the jail door of said county, one NEGRO MAN named William, aged between 35 and 40 years, levied upon as the property of one J. Brooks, and sold to satisfy judicials No 107 to November term 1841, in favor of Richard M. Warring.

"ALEXANDER HUNTER,
"Marshall District Columbia."

Yours judiciously,
SAM WELLER.

# *TOCSIN OF LIBERTY*,

## November 3, 1842

*Smallwood congratulates Torrey, now* Tocsin's *editor, for leaving Washington and insists that "Sam Weller" is neither Torrey nor Abel Brown. He offers faux sympathy for the "Patriarchs" whose enslaved workers keep fleeing north, including a physician, a butcher, and the bureaucrat in charge of public gardens, and rails at another for claiming he has no idea why they left him. He tells the story of James Burgess and threatens to expose a slaveholder if Burgess's wife is not freed.*

### MORE FLEEING FROM HAPPINESS.

Washington, D.C.

October 22, 1842

Mr. Editor.—My father and I are very glad to see you safe out of the hands of the Philistines![1] I should have sent a letter to your paper before, but I have been waiting to get some particular facts which I now send you. By the way, I want you to assure the good people in Albany, and thereabouts, that Samivel Weller, jr., and Abel Brown are neither kith, kin, nor acquaintance.[2] And the date of my letter will assure Mister Fuller that *you* and I are very different people. Strange that he ever mistook a yankee for me! How I laughed when his son Ned came home from Boston, Albany and elsewhere, with a flea in his ear, just as wise about that "boy Henson," as he was before he spent so much money in the chase. Why couldn't he believe my letter that said Henson was in Canada? I rather reckon he must look *me* up before he gets the real state of the case; for I'm an *old settler*, here: and I know the *rich man* in whose stable Henson was hid, the day he left, till after dark. He don't live a thousand miles from F street! I hope you will expose Mr. A. Fuller's treatment of you. What business had he to threaten and swagger at you, swearing like a pirate: and to give you 12 hours to leave the city, or he and some *gentlemen*, forsooth, would *force* you out! [I have concluded to spare Mr. Fuller, vile as his conduct was, out of regard to his family and friends. ED. TOCSIN.] Give it to him, strong! There's a peck of trouble among the Patriarchs,[3] in this city, since you left. I want to comfort the dear souls a little, by assuring them that their absent friends have all reached Canada, in safety, having been seen in Toronto, and some of them have written back to me, in this city, that their relations might be assured of their health and good prospects.

It *was* wery cruel, *wery*, in Peter Matthews to run off to Canada, after his sweet, swearing master had paid $100 for catching him only 6 weeks before! Poor James Larned! Why did you listen to your tender hearted wife? Had you sold him when he first come back, your money would have been safe. But alas, there is no hope for you! Peter is in Toronto. He loved a certain bright eyed Sophy Jackson even better than his dear master; and Sophy you know, left Washington a year ago, on the grand tour! If you are really rich enough to pay the second cool hundred out of your salary as Clerk, it would only be fair to send it to Peter. For he lost nearly that when he jumped into the water, from the bridge, where your man-hunters headed him off, on his first attempt to get to Canada, by way of Frederick. Will you do it?

Surely Job's trials were nothing to those of poor NOTLEY MADDOX. I will copy his last advertisement from the Intelligencer. I wonder the editor did not condole with him!

> "RUNAWAYS—One thousand and fifty dollars reward.—I have not heard from mine, as advertised in the National Intelligencer during September past. In addition to those therein described and named, my young lad called HANSON, and sometimes FRANK, left me on the night of the 26th ultimo. He is a mulatto, rather dark, about 20 years

old, common size, moderate intellect; took away a black cloth coat, other clothing not recollected. He has been often sent to the Washington market with vegetables. I have now five males and one female that have left me *without cause known to me.*

For their arrest and confinement in any jail so that I can get them again, I will give two hundred dollars each for the men, if taken in a free State; and fifty for the woman; or one half, no matter where taken. Forged certificates of freedom, with good imitations of official seals, are common.

"NOTLEY MADDOX

"NEAR WASHINGTON, D.C."

Notley is mistaken about the "official seals." They are all good ones, for God gave them, in stamping MANHOOD on the brow of his poor slaves. He is a booby to advertise the slaves who went to Canada years ago. Hanson, the "young lad" of "20 years old," happens to think himself a man! and so he went to the Springs, and sprung over to Canada! and "SAM," alias, Mr. Samuel Johnson, has been there these two months. A witty fellow, Sam is! I don't wonder, Mr. Maddox, that you mourn $200 worth of tears and sighs for his company. He would force a smile on the granite face of the "old man of the mountain," that I saw once, in the Franconia Notch, up in New Hampshire! I *must* say, Notley Maddox, if you insult the nation again, by pretending that your six slaves left you "without any cause known to you," that I shall be obliged to expose your *cruelty* to them; your robbing them of liberty and property, was quite bad enough. But it hurts my feelings to write about your violent temper, and tyrannical conduct and it *might hurt* yours to have it known! You may make yourself easy about Frank. He went to Canada, direct.

Mr. JAMES MAHER, the public gardener,[4] must regret to lose the company of Margaret Myers, and I don't doubt he does—But Uncle Sam pays him so much money for nothing, that he can afford the pecuniary loss, very well. Doubtless, Mr. Maher's conscience has never been *quite* easy, since he killed that slave in his barn with the piece of old cart tire. Let him remember that a *white witness still lives, who was not present at his trial.* I don't wonder Margaret wanted to leave him, if all I have heard of his conduct to poor laboring *white* people is true! Why does this man never employ an AMERICAN laborer on the public grounds? Perhaps they would [not] submit so quietly to his hard conditions!

Dr. WM. H. GUNNELL, down there by the wharf, is a 'cute one, sure enough. How many times have I heard him boast that "no nigger could ever get away from him!" Ah, you're not so wise as you thought for; *or* Mrs. Tilly could never have taken her child out of your very bed room! On reflection, don't you think it was cruel, Dr. Gunnell, to make that little child, only five years old, lie on your chamber floor, and keep awake to tend your own *white* baby, while you and your wife slept? Don't you think it was wrong to treat that Christian mother as a mere "breeding wench" and refuse her husband for *months* together, all access to her society? If you have a mind to confess your wrong to Mrs. Tilly, and pay DENNIS SHAW his wages, and make his double and twisted eyes sparkle, I will give you a letter to them, on application at the office of the "underground railroad."

JAMES BURGESS and his sister Eliza, (and her child) wish to assure their tender hearted mistress that they are well and happy in Queen Vic's dominions.[5] Perhaps her son-in-law, Mr. Francis Markoe, can comfort her widowed heart; if not, I don't know who can. James, before he left, wished me to write a few things about his story for some northern paper. Be it known, then, that James has been cook in the U.S. Navy Yard, in this city, for eight years. He was enlisted contrary to law, as the officers of the yard well knew. His mistress received $18 a month for his services, and never allowed him *one cent* of it for his own. True, the regulations of the Navy Yard compelled her to keep him well clothed. His mistress went to the Warrenton Springs this summer, and authorised James to receive his last three months wages, which fell due in her absence. James very naturally thought that the best use he could make of his earnings was to take a trip to Saratoga with his dear sister, for their health, and when they were *so near* Canada, they doubtless found it pleasant to cross the line, just to see a few old acquaintances. That sister of his well deserves his care and love, for she was a second mother to him in his childhood. He will pay her by watching over her fatherless child.

How James' whole frame quivered when he told me the story of his wife's being whipped on her naked back with the rawhide in his presence! She is nearly 25 years old, and at 25 is entitled to beg her liberty. Her tyrant master, Mr. F——g M——, lives just off from the old road to Bladensburg, in Maryland. James could never go see his wife except on Sundays. One Sunday in order to aggravate his feelings, the old tyrant chose to tie up his wife to a tree to flog her, just as James got there. James saw four or five blows inflicted, but he could bear no more. He cut her loose, and when the master undertook to punish him for it, James gave the old tyrant a sound beating, and fled. The next morning the woman whipper came to the Navy Yard in a great rage, and demanded that James should be severely punished. The Lieutenant of the yard was disposed to gratify him, but James claimed a trial by court martial, utterly denying that he had violated any rule of the service; for he was absent on leave, and was out of the district. The officer scolded; but he knew that the *enlistment of a slave*, contrary to law, might cost him his commission, if the matter came to trial, so James was let off with a reprimand. If the old woman-whipper don't let his wife go to Canada next summer, I will expose him, *by name*, if I remain in Washington, as I expect to; for it's a satisfaction I cannot forego to show up the deeds of darkness in our capital. How the wounded *do* flutter! They are great ninnies to suppose that such abolitionists as yourself and Leavitt[6] would run any risk to ship off their slaves, when you are doing so much more in other ways to put down slavery. I can tell them better. Why, there's a rich lawyer in this city, a slaveholder, who does a deed of mercy in that way at times. Pro-slavery members of Congress do it often out of mere humanity. Besides, a shrewd slave *has wit enough at any time* to get round a lazy, mole-eyed slaveholder. Even the Fullers lost so much of their Yankee 'cuteness by becoming slaveholders, that HENSON disappeared from before their face and eyes in the middle of the afternoon, when three of them were watching him!

☛ Now I wish all these gentry to take notice that their slaves get off just as fast now, while all the abolitionists they suspected of aiding them are absent, as they did last Spring, when they were here. ☛ And another thing. ☛ Here am I, SAMUEL WELLER, jun., still in the city to scourge and mock at them, and defy all their puny efforts to discover me, or the "underground railroad."

Perhaps Mr. PHILIP OTTERBACK, one of our principal butchers, a German by birth, is "chief mourner" after the long procession of runaways. It was a cool $600 out of his pocket to lose Edward Brooks, "my negro man Ned Brooks," as his advertisements in the papers call him. I presume Ned, being a capital butcher, thought it became an enterprising young man, like him, to set up for himself, and as he wanted a woman to *try out the fat* for him, who could he take better than his charming little wife? Mrs. Brooks wishes to be remembered to Mr. D. C. Croft, whose kindness, and that of the family, she gratefully speaks of in her letter. She would not have left them, but for her husband's sake, and she thanks them for not advertising her: it would have hurt her feelings to have her name put in the papers in such a way.

But Mr. Philip Otterback, doubtless, mourns the loss of his darling Betsey Williams, far more than that of Ned Brooks. People *do* say that Philip loved Betsey a little better than Mrs. Otterback altogether approved of. Betsey is a noble girl. Bought, when a child, for a *certain purpose*, and trained up under his eye, it was provoking to find her virtue so stern as to repel her master with scorn. Nay, to jump out of her chamber window when the intruder kicked in the door! Happily, the vigilance of a wife and son will sometimes prevent the evil intended by the head of the family. If Mr. Otterback ever becomes a widower, and will come to Toronto a courting in an honorable way, perhaps Betsey will relent. It was sad to see how dejected he looked in the market for weeks after it. Perhaps he can spare a few tears by way of sympathy with Mrs. McKune and her son-in-law, the Hon. Virgil Maxcy, late Minister to Holland, on the loss of George and John Turner, two as fine fellows as ever lived; too white, by many shades, to pass for "niggers" any where but in a slaveholding city. When Canada is a free Republic they will be her boldest soldiers.

But I must cease for the present, or I shall not have room in my letter for a few little incidents worth naming.

The other day I was at the Rail Road Depot, when Dr. Gunnell, with Patten, the constable, (a mean fellow,) were there. Some one said to Gunnell—

"Why Doctor, I thought you and DENNIS were like brothers! They say he's left you!"

The Doctor replied, "If Dennis should come back to-morrow I would trust him to the Bank with $1000, as soon as any one." Patten, pointing over to Mrs. ——'s,[7] said, "It was that fellow over yonder, that helped him off," (mentioning your name!*) "I've had a warrant out against him for a fortnight, but could never catch him. I sent —— to Mrs ———'s after him.—That d—d old b—h was as guilty as he."

The poor manstealers and their watchdogs are greatly at a loss to know how their victims escape. At times they watch the Rail Road, with eagle eyes.—But men and women *do* go off in the cars before the faces of Suit, Thorn and other wretches like them,[8] very often. "Their eyes are holden,"[9] as a slave said once, "so that they see the poor fugitive."

At other times they reckon their victims escape in coaches or wagons. Then they imagine they go by water, which is often the case. All this shows that they would give a *plum* to know where the under-ground Rail Road begins! That name was given to it by constable ZELL of Baltimore.[10]

Have you forgotten a certain Walter W. W. Bowie, who made two very violent and vulgar speeches in the great Slaveholders'

*I call on Patten for an explanation.—I never avoided him or any one. I passed him daily, the last fortnight I was in the city. I believe his talk of the warrant was a coward's bravado over an absent man.—ED. TOCSIN.

Convention at Annapolis[11] last winter; and who helped get up the mob against you? A few days ago he sold to one of our city traders SEVEN slaves—two men, two women and three well grown lads, all for $1300 only! Less than $186, a piece! Five years ago they were worth $5000. Some one asked him why he sold them? He replied, "niggers were running away so fast he meant to have something for his, while he could get it!" Gunnell and Otterback have both declared they never meant to have any more slaves! "Sour grapes," I reckon. An attempt was made, recently, to find out the way a certain slave escaped by intercepting the correspondence of our colored people. But the upright delivering clerk, Mr. TREE would not listen to it at all. He deserves credit for it.

I must close my letter without paying my respects to the large number who have recently been afflicted by the loss of their beloved servants! The conductor of the "U. G. R. Road" tells me that over 20 have gone, this month! You may depend on hearing from them, through me, as soon as I learn of their reaching the other end of their journey!

Yours, in hatred of slavery,

SAMUEL WELLER, Jr.

P. S. My father writes me that Boz DICKENS, in his new work on America,[12] abuses this country shockingly. I'm sorry we let him write our Biography. For this is a glorious land after all, if the curse of slavery could be removed. Pa says, the way Boz shows up the slaveholders is a caution to snakes! What a capital subject for him to show up, in a novel! How MEAN he'd make the robbers of the poor look! Slaveholders are worse than Ralph Nickleby, or even the old Jew, in Oliver Twist!

Yours, SAM.

# *TOCSIN OF LIBERTY,*

## November 17, 1842

*Smallwood introduces a new imaginary character, Samivel Weller's nephew Joshua, who is organizing escapes from the Pittsburgh area. Likely he is referring to a real ally in the underground railroad, but it is hard to say who it might be. He stretches to the antic breaking point the metaphor of "the business of transporting humanity" and talks about a breakout of the enslaved from slave trader William Williams's notorious private jail in Washington. He makes a first mention of a pseudonymous "son," Samivel Weller III, but this character will disappear after the next letter.*

### Interesting Correspondence.

Pittsburgh

October 29, 1842

Dear Uncle Sam:—I am happy to inform you, that I have been enabled to enter into a partnership with John Goodwill and Co., and have the prospect of doing well in the business of transporting humanity. The firm takes the name of Joshua Weller and Co.[1] We have had a pretty good run of business since we commenced. We have shipped for Queen Victoria's dominions five fine fellows, and if their Virginia, Tennessee, and Kentucky masters will call at our office, we will tell them, free gratis for nothing, where they may find these noble fellows. And we have had on hand a mixed lot of *seven*, which we have disposed of handsomely. I will give you a particular account of our business in my next, the object of this being only to let you and the public know, that we are prepared to ship, in good style, and on the shortest notice, all humanity that may be committed to our care.

Your loving nephew,

JOSHUA WELLER

*To Uncle Sam Weller, Albany, New York*

P. S. Will your papers please copy, as we want it known that we can do things right, and nobody needn't be afraid to commit their business to us.

Washington, D.C.

November 9, 1842

My dear Nevy—The printer at Albany sent me the Spirit of Liberty, printed at Pittsburgh, that had the letter of your'n in it, announcing your co-partnership with a fine company in the business of "shipping humanity." I don't know when I've felt so proud of our family since Boz writ the biography of myself and pa. It will be a great consolation to your venerable Pa, and mine to reflect that you do so much credit to the bringing up you received. I am happy to see in Mr. Boz's new book (American Notes), that he gives the mean people who plunder the poor of their hard earnings, and claim the aid of the law to help them, something like their just deserts.

One thing I must say, that these people will never thank your Firm for information where their "contented and happy" property has gone to, unless you will set the human blood hounds on the track, and shout "*stuboy!*"[2] I have been cused not a little, because I got them printers in Albany to send such information to my neighbors in *these* diggins.

In order to encourage your trade (seeing as you're my Nevy, and the very image of your departed mother, sister Content), I will speak to the conductors of the moveable underground railroad about giving you a quarter of their custom. This will give you a fair start, and your own enterprise, and the skill and humanity of your partners must do the rest. It will comfort your heart to know that 36 more bales of human hopes, fears, joys, and sympathies, have been forwarded by my house from this city, since my last letter was writ to the Tocsin. They were worth in the cattle market (just in front of the Capitol and President's house; you remember I showed it to you last summer), at least $10,000, at the present low prices. Our *way* freight, in Maryland, has also been considerable. The fall and winter supplies are not yet half forwarded. When I have a little more leisure, you will see the *bills of lading* in the papers. You will be charmed, Joshua, to find, in the course of your trade, how little wit it needs to outwit a slaveholder. I am about starting for *central* Virginia, nigh on to Carolina, to get a few choice articles for a particular market in Canada. The roads are in fine condition, and our gains (in humble prayers, heartfelt thanks, and the blessings of the poor) are very great. Be careful about *your agents* in the south. I have been very much troubled lately to find some of mine *fleecing* the poor fugitives. They learned it of slaveholders. The whole paternity of manhunters was thrown into a fever, last week, by the escape of several men from Williams' Pen,[3] or cattle market, on Maryland Avenue. They were citizens of this region, sold to the trader, and put there for safe keeping till the next slave ship sailed for New Orleans, "and a market." There were many hearts in this city that rejoiced in their escape. The papers utter loud complaints on the rapid progress of our business. I helped the brave fellows out by the loan of a file and hammer, with an old chisel. If the Washingtonians would follow the example of the Bashaw of Tunis, and destroy the slave barracoons,[4] half the nation would come on a pilgrimage to see the ruins. God bless you, dear Nevy, and prosper your trade.

I am, your loving Uncle,

SAMUEL WELLER, Jr.

P. S. I send this letter to them printers in Albany, because the publication of it will serve to make our business known, and get us custom. Those who advertise freely always find their account in it. And as Col. Stone, of the N.Y. Commercial, and his Washington correspondent, Mr. James Frederick Otis (the recreant signer of the declaration of sentiments, in 1833,[5] who repudiated his abolition to save his sweet neck from a lynch halter, down in Virginia) will both see this letter, I may add a little for their special benefit.

Mr. Otis complained bitterly, some days ago, of the sad fate of a patriarch about ten miles from this city, whose naughty slaves would not fulfill their "promise" to go to Missouri with him! Naughty creatures to love LIBERTY better than their "dear Massa!" Well, some of them *were* naughty; though it was as much their misfortune as their fault. For their kind master never taught them to read the Bible, or anything about TEMPERANCE, either by example or precept. So, some of them, when they got here, took too much liquor, in one of the accursed grog shops, kept by a white man, and got drunk. They were seized, and placed in Williams' Pen for safe keeping. These were the men that *broke out*, to whom I referred before. It was a good temperance lecture to them, and you won't catch them in a *white man's liquid fire shop* again. I never see faults in the uneducated slaves, without charging them to the bad example of white men, involuntarily. If the colored people had their rights, and were treated AS MEN, their guilt would be far greater than it is. The *free* people of color, even here, rise above the oppressions that have crushed them, and, as a general thing, do well.

I may as well tell you, now that I think some of putting my son, Samivel Weller, 3d into business in Albany, in company with a few other choice spirits, who have long been engaged there on their own hook, but sadly need more cash capital, and one of OUR WELLERS to aid them!

Your Uncle,

SAM.

# *TOCSIN OF LIBERTY,*

## December 1, 1842

*Smallwood's escape operation seems to be accelerating, and he uses numbered points for the first time to be able to keep straight some fifteen slaveholders and at least nineteen people who have escaped them. He shows off his inside knowledge of the enslavers' doings: who used a red-hot key to brand an enslaved man, who had a secret plan to sell a man south to New Orleans, who paid a police constable to hunt fruitlessly for a runaway. He rails at a slaveholder who implies that the man who escaped from him has no real last name, though he uses one.*

Washington, D.C.

November 19

Mr. Printer:—

I have finally made up my mind not to set up my son Samivel 3d in business in your city, till the spring business is about to open. Then we shall be able to answer, through him and my dear Nevy Joshua, all orders for *free* or *paid* labor that may be handed in.

I have to comfort quite a large number of afflicted patriarchs, which I will strive to do, *after my manner.* If they don't find comfort in what I write, it must be because they are not duly submissive to the mysterious providence, by which so many valuable chattels are snatched from them, and turned into men!

1. I wish to say a word to my old friend, JOHN HARRY, of Georgetown, D.C., and I won't think of taking for it over $100 of the $200 he offers for the recovery of "his two servants!"

☛ Messrs. Slade, Giddings, Crafts and other boarders at Mrs. Sprigg's,[1] last session, will not be sorry to learn that their favorite waiter, JOHN DOUGLASS, and his younger brother Lewis have escaped from "massa Harry's" grasp, and are free!—The pleasure of gratifying so many good men, must be a comfort to Mr. Harry, under his losses! If John Harry had the least regard to human sympathies, the voice of conscience or the commands of Jehovah, he would send John Douglass' young wife and children after him, at his own expense. But he is in his nature a *tyrant* though in Georgetown he passes for a respectable man! I tell him, that I, Samivel Weller, junior, never see him strut by the President's house, or roll along in his carriage, without despising him for the *meanness* of living on the unrequited labor of the poor! Comfort him! I would that the same lash *his victims* have endured, might fall on his back! Hear what he says of these two fine young men, one of them about as white as he.

> "JOHN and LEWIS; they are brothers—John is about twenty-three years of age, near six feet high, stout and well made; is a first-rate house servant; by trade is a white-washer; he is a mulatto, perhaps may be called copper colored; his voice is strong and speaks plenty quick. Lewis is two years younger, about five feet six or eight inches high, brighter in color than John; stammers very much at times; is also stout. They have each a good suit of clothes, but color not recollected. It is very probable that they have forged free papers; they are both quite intelligent, having been much employed as waiters in genteel families."

They "forged" no free papers, sir!—God gave them the right to be free, and they took it. They went by the GREAT NATIONAL UNDERGROUND RAIL ROAD!—"Thy prey hath escaped thee!"

2. I love to prove how "pure and undefiled" my religion is, by "visiting the widows," "in their affliction;" though I never had occasion to comfort one, as many yankees do, widows who

are endowed with a large lot of slaves; "marrying the slaves with the woman annexed," as the Southerners often phrase it. But I *did* call on Mrs. SUSAN HOLMEAD,[2] to condole with her of the loss of Richard Hawkins. She keeps a capital boarding house, on the Avenue, close by to where I live. But she is aware how much of the comfort of her house depended on Dick, for she would give $200 to see his almost *white* face again. She gives a lady's description of him:

> "Dick is a bright mulatto, aged about 24, about 5 feet 7 or 8 inches high, straight black hair, blue eyes, has a defect in his front teeth somewhat affecting his speech, has a slight limp in his gait, which is scarcely perceptible unless noticed particularly."

Ah, neither you, nor your pimping "agent," C. H. James, will ever look on Richard's manly features again! Poor Susan! It *was* affecting to hear you speak of your situation as a "lone" widder, and to hear you tell of the $800 taken from your children's mouths! But it affected me *still more* to think of *your guilt*, as a female tyrant, plundering a poor, helpless man of his hard earnings! *That* was what made me weep, when you so gratefully thought I was sympathizing with you!

3. Another widder! How often I think of my Pa's emphatic caution, "Samivel," says he, "Samivel, beware of widders!" How impressively he held up his little finger, and cocked his second best hat on one side, when he said it! I thought of it when the U. G. Railroad agent told me that Josiah Galloway, had left widder Susan G. Bell, who lives on Capitol Hill, because he wanted liberty, and that the widder was about to sell him to the traders. Ah, "beware of widders! they're always wicious creatures!" Mrs. Bell, 150 dollars will never get Josiah within the sound of your clapper again!

4. As my friend Truman Cross "damned the pock-marked face" of Charles Burgess, and has had the good sense to refrain

from spending his money in advertising him, it is to be presumed that he is not so much sorry to *lose him*, as *mad* at the loss of his money. Charles is a fine fellow, nevertheless, and in his last letter to me wished to be remembered to his *boss*.

5. Mr. John F. Cox is entitled to equal praise in allowing his loss of Nathan Southard to pass *sub silentio*.[3] And if he had not sent that sneaking, slave-catching constable after him, he might have saved his *money* too! It was no go.

6. Mr. James Long has a long head; so he sent a flaming handbill to Philadelphia, with a full description of his fugitive chattel, William Harris. But nobody would stick it up! Bill told my son, up in the north, that he laughed over his boss' description of himself, which a friend in Philadelphia showed him, not a little. It will be a *long* time, Mr. Long, before your long head will lengthen out your crooked soul enough to grasp at the abstract idea of a *man*, or a man's right to his own body and soul.

7. Lewis Hawkins *really* shed tears when he spoke of leaving Mr. George Wilson, a clerk in the Treasury, (land office) and his kind-hearted wife. But, with every disposition to acknowledge their *uniform kindness and affection to him and* his family, especially when his former wife and children were gambled away by that scoundrel ______ M______; he still cannot any longer recognize *their right* to take from him $120 a year of his hard earnings. Words of kindness don't make the robbery any less real; his *own* wife and children need the money, especially to educate his children. He means to send his oldest boy to college, which all Mr. & Mrs. Wilson's kindness would never have enabled him to do. Let them send their own roguish son to college, and *see* which has the brightest talents!

8. John Fitzcheu thought he had done marketing enough for Mr. Joshua Pierce, and therefore determined to emigrate to a land of freedom, and set up a garden of his own, near to some large town. Who can blame him?

9. The same general idea of setting up for himself had long been floating in the mind of Stephen Brown. So Steve thought Massa Pruce might seek for another "nigger" to do his dirty work without pay.

10. Two brothers, Hannibal Hall and Robert Hall, wish to assure their masters how much they regretted to leave their service. But they loved freedom. Hannibal says he can't pretend to vie with Capt. E. in military prowess, but he can *out-general* him at any time! And Robert wishes Mr. Henry Tollson to understand that *family secrets* are apt to leak out; and he had no idea of going to New Orleans.

11. The manifold afflictions of Patriarch *Notley Maddox*, I have frequently had occasion to speak of. I must add to the same catalogue the loss of Frank Hanson. My sympathy with him in his *seventh* loss, in so short a time is too deep for words!

12. Lawrence Paine begs to say to Esq. Fendall,[4] that if he *is* smart enough to be district attorney, he isn't quiet enough to catch a slave who wants his freedom! And he has never forgotten or forgiven the brutality that *branded* him on the hand, in 1840, with a red hot door key, to *mark* him! Pretty fellow this Fendall is for a public officer, or for a lawyer to please the cause of justice and mercy! Shame on the cowardly, passionate tyrant, who disgraces the name of "democrat!" Ugh!

13. I must now turn and pay my respects to a very great tyrant, WASHINGTON BERRY. His three men, for whom he offers $1,000 reward, will never again have their backs scored up with the whip of his overseer, while one who dishonors the name of the humane *Washington* stands by and cries, "harder! lick the life out of the d——d dogs!" If all the blood spilt on his farm turned *blue*, it might be called "Blue Plains"[5] sure enough. Mr. Berry may save his $500 for the "forgers of their passes," as they had none! Had they desired any, *perhaps* a county clerk of his acquaintance would not have refused a

*genuine seal* for $30 or so! If Mr. Berry would not stand on the roll of infamy with Fielding Maginder and other monsters, he must be careful how he talks and acts.

14. Again, W. H. Edes says his man "Bill, who *calls himself* William Martin," has "gone off without the least provocation." J. Y. Young has lost "negro man William, who *calls himself* William Hall."

What should they "call themselves?" Because *slaveholders* allow their victims *no family name*, in order to accustom the people to the denial of their *family relations*, is that any reason why *they should unman themselves* and forget the ties of nature and of love? Oh how thoroughly the accursed system strikes at the root of every thing *noble*, just and humane! My paper is full, yet I have not told one-half the trouble of the patriarchs. I have some things of great importance to tell you in my next. Yours, for liberty,

SAM WELLER, Jr.

# *TOCSIN OF LIBERTY*,

## December 8, 1842

*Smallwood, briefly dropping his madcap style, raises the alarm about a treaty with Britain that may create a legal pretext for American slaveholders to demand the return of people who have escaped to Canada. He claims that between March and December, some 150 people have escaped from Washington with his help, inflicting a loss of $75,000, about $2.6 million in 2024 dollars. He denounces a new city jail, used to lock up runaways, and delights in the attacks on slavery in Dickens's new* American Notes.

☛ATROCIOUS CONSPIRACY!☚

Washington, D.C.

November 19, 1842

Mr. Editor:

I have many things to say this week, but the most important matter I will mention first. It is a matter sufficiently alarming to the friends of liberty. I was afraid at the time of it, that there was some secret in the 10th article of Lord Ashburton's treaty,[1] which binds the two governments to give up fugitive *felons*, for two years. It is true, that it requires an act of the British Parliament to give validity to the treaty. Whether that will be given, or in what form, we shall know before long. The British Abolitionists won't be caught napping on this subject.

While the negotiations were going on, I, Samivel Weller, junior, was not an idle spectator. I knew that DANIEL WEBSTER had never recovered from the *stroke* he received "under that

October sun," at Richmond. I knew that President Tyler felt a *natural* anxiety about his two *almost* white sons,[2] Charles and John, who left him *without leave*, two or three years ago. He might wish to get them back to his paternal bosom, even if he had to resort to subterfuge, to do it!

☛ The Lord Ashburton, himself, was an old slave-holder in the West Indies, and received a large slice of the "compensation" money that was wrung out of the sweat of the poor of Great Britain, under pretence of paying the planters for the loss of their slave property!

An old slave-holder's sympathies were not very likely to be on the right side, even if he *don't* own any slaves in this country, as I more than suspect he does! Besides, I have reason to believe that Calhoun and others in the secrets of the slaveholder's plans,[3] were well satisfied that under this treaty there would be a way of preventing fugitive slaves from having a home in Canada.

My letters, and other sources of information, have made you aware of the large number that has escaped from this den of robbers, the past year, by means of our new underground rail road. The perfect secrecy and quickness with which they escaped, baffling the most experienced hunters, the shrewdest police officers, and the most active, discerning, watchful masters, have greatly alarmed the nabobs, and my comments have made them feel exceedingly sore, respecting it. They felt themselves in a *fix*. Swearing only made the matter worse. In half their sneering, laughing neighbors, they suspected they saw me, Samivel Weller, and often charged men accordingly—but all to no purpose. The railroad went on, and the slaves became free, and their purses suffered to an amazing extent. In the single form of runaway slaves, reckoning them at $500 apiece, the District of Columbia has been taxed not less than $75,000 since March last! In any other form, such a tax would make a rebellion! I mean to tax them twice that, next year!

But, alarmed at their losses, and despairing of discovering the mode in which their chattels became *men*, they have devised a plan, by which they think *that treaty* may be available for their purposes.

☛ So they have united in a plan to induce the GOVERNOR GENERAL OF CANADA *to give up their fugitives*, AS FELONS! They have individually made affidavits before magistrates, charging the fugitives with thefts of clothing, money and other articles, to an amount sufficient to send them to jail.

☛ Next, the plotters got the endorsement, as I have reason to believe, of DANIEL WEBSTER, Secretary of State, to their affidavits. On this foundation, the proper officers of this District, the Judges of the District Court, have demanded the surrender of these *felons*, under the late Treaty.

☛ Then the plotters made up a heavy purse, and sent one WILLIAM MILLER, of this city (brother of Dr. Miller) to Canada, with a power of attorney, from each of them, to *demand* the surrender of these fugitives. I have written to the British minister here, Mr. Fox, stating the facts, and also to the Governor General, Sir Charles Bagot, to warn him of the nature of this infamous conspiracy of the slaveholders and slave-catchers of this city and Georgetown, to break up the only home of freedom on the northern half of this continent. I would suggest that you, Gerrit Smith, A. Stewart, Joshua Leavitt,[4] and others, should also address him on the subject. The matter is too grave and all-important for trifling, and I have therefore dropped somewhat of my usual style in speaking of it. This infamous plan to bend the Treaty to the purposes of slavery, *must be defeated*, at all hazards. If the Treaty *is* to be so used, the sooner we know it, the better.

I wish also to call public attention in the north, to the use of the *new jail*, in this city, which, you remember, stands a hundred rods north-west of the capitol, over Goose Creek, or "Tiber," as the classical folks call it. Most of the northern people that cross it are *made geese*, by the slaveholders! The people of the free states were taxed by Congress to build this new jail, to the amount of nearly $75,000, and it is nothing but a PEN to *confine slaves both for* SALE, and to prevent their running away! It is now freely used for both purposes.

Chaney, a messenger in the capitol, put a young girl in, a few nights ago, who has only a limited time to serve! He was afraid she would run away! Such facts take place, daily!

I am happy to add that the men who broke out of Williams' pen, have never been heard of here. [They have been *here*—they are safe!—*Ed. Tocsin*]

The way "Dickens' Notes" gall the slave-holders, here, is curious to see!—They flattered and soaped him so much, last summer, as you will remember, that they really thought he was agoing to use the "peculiar institutions" very gently! The way they curse him, is awful! Why, didn't they introduce him to the floor of the House, as much as Lord Morpeth, or Ashburton! But the *true Democrat* was not to be caught by such chaff! If Pa's life and mine was to be writ over again a thousand times, nobody but Boz should do it!

Yours, for liberty,

SAM. WELLER, JR.

# *TOCSIN OF LIBERTY*,

## December 15, 1842

*Smallwood attacks the Auxiliary Guard, a new police unit in Washington, claiming that it is failing to prevent crime because it is so intent on harassing and exploiting Black residents. And he criticizes the Post Office for allowing a slaveholder, Dr. William Gunnell, to examine private correspondence of African Americans. He claims to have witnessed Gunnell's rage as he read an earlier copy of* Tocsin of Liberty, *mailed to him by the editors, describing the escape of the people he enslaved.*

### THE AUXILIARY GUARD—THE POST OFFICE

Washington, D.C.

November 15, 1842

Mr. Editor:

I am on a sort of watchtower, I often think, and I note with keen interest the transactions both here, at the south, where despotism reigns supreme, and among your pure hills and valleys—I perceive by the returns that the whigs are defeated, both in New York and Massachusetts. And no marvel, when we consider how they have betrayed their promises to the people. I have not a particle of sympathy with the *locofocraçy*:[1] they are only more open and manly enemies of human liberty. But I did think that the Whig Reform Party of 1840 would not utterly fail to redeem their engagements to the dear people!

But I wish to call attention to one of the measures of the present Whig Congress, which may be compared with their past pledges of regard for human rights. I refer to the famous

AUXILIARY GUARD,[2]

established to protect this city from incendiaries and robbers, and to keep the public property safe, *and* for other—not named, purposes.

☛ There have been more stores broken open, and more incendiary attempts, since the Guard was established, than for many years before, in the same space of time! Do you ask why this is so?

The answer is easy. ☛ The Guard, instead of doing their duty, have been prowling about, searching the houses of colored people in search of fugitive slaves, that they may get the reward offered for them! This fact they cannot deny.

It is right that the people of the Free States should know for what purposes their Representatives have taxed them with the support of this infamous Guard, in the Nation's Capital.

The most active of this crew are COX and LITTLE. The other night one of them started a woman out of the house in which she lived, because, it was said that she was from Alexandria, and had no free papers. She run into a *fodder* house, [barn] in which a slave was concealed, for the purpose of effecting his escape from one of the most cruel masters in Maryland, THOMAS BERRY of Prince George's Co. The poor fellow was alarmed, ran out of the fodder house, and of course they caught him. Cox will get $50 for his share of the reward, besides his $30 a month from the Government.

You are aware of the city law, requiring the watch to take up colored people who are found in the streets after 10 o'clock at night. The pale faced rowdies want the streets to themselves, after that hour! The colored people are so generally within doors, after that hour, that it is a matter of great regret, on the part of the watch, they lose their fees! So they talk of limiting the time of the colored people to 9 o'clock! No colored person can pass after 10 o'clock, no matter how respectable he is, unless he is a tool in their hands to betray his own color. This then, is a most important part of the duty of the Auxiliary Guard, which a *Whig Congress* imposed upon us, and to sustain which they tax the people $7500 a year!

I would call attention to the rascality practiced in our city

POST OFFICE.

I had occasion, some time ago, to commend Mr. FREE, the delivering clerk, for refusing to trample on his oath, and the laws of the land, by allowing other people to open letters directed to the people of color.

Recently, Dr. WM. H. GUNNELL received a copy of your paper containing my poor attempts to comfort him under the weight of afflictions quite enough to break the heart of any Patriarch! He was, strange to say, quite furious with me. How I laughed at him, as I stood by his side, one day, and heard him sputter, in connection with some gentlemen in the market! He was ready to eat up alive your humble servant, Sam Weller, jr. if he only knew who he was!

Well, this worthy thought to discover the whereabouts of his lost chattels, if he could examine the letters at the Post office for our colored citizens. So he went to Dr. Jones, the P. M.[3] and with great difficulty, got leave to open them, by *putting his name to them*! One of them was for Dennis Smallwood, the coachman. It happened to come from the Hon. ABBOT LAWRENCE, of Boston! You remember that Mr. Lawrence was one of the gentlemen who helped Dennis get his freedom. The story is worth telling. Dennis had more chance to earn money than almost any slave in this city. In the course of years, by iron industry, he had hoarded up $1000. He offered his master, Mr. O, (who lives near the depot, you recollect) the whole sum for his freedom. But he was such *profitable plunder*, that the old tyrant would not hear a word of it. So Dennis made known his case to Mr. Lawrence, and other members of Congress, and they found means to send him to Boston, without Mr. O's particular consent! (It was about two years before we began to build the under ground Railroad!) The master knew not where he was, till after the session closed. Then he received a very polite letter from Mr. Lawrence, stating that Dennis had authorised him to offer Mr. O. the $1000 still, if he would send him on his free papers. Mr. O. was very glad to comply. Dennis came back here, and did well. He now owns his two coaches and horses, and is very much respected. His wife is still a slave, as you know. She is a very amiable woman. The other two letters opened by Gunnell, were directed to one of the Brook's, and came from relations of theirs.———

☛ Let the people in New Bedford, Mass., look out for kidnappers, about these times!

Now I would like to know if the fact that Dr. Jones made Gunnell write his name on these letters exonerates him from blame, for violating his oath of office, respecting the safe delivery of letters to the person to whom they are directed? Is slavery to be suffered, for the vilest ends, to maintain a system of *espionage* over the Post office? Is the law to be trampled under foot, in WASHINGTON, with impunity? What say the Post office Committee of the House; I appeal to the chairman, Hon. Mr. BRIGGS,[4] to summon Dr. Jones, and Wm. H. Gunnell, before the committee, and inquire into this atrocious violation of the sacredness of the U.S. Mail, and of the laws of the Union. Will he dare act on the principle that the rights of the people may be trampled down, if their skins happen to be *about* as dark as his? Or will he remember the time when hard labor in the blacksmith shop bronzed his manly face, and strive to do justice to his poor brethren in this city? As he is about to retire from public life, let him ask, "how can I close my career more honorably, than by a vindication of the rights of the poor?" He will find ready coadjutors in Messrs. Adams, Gates, Giddings, Slade, Ramsay,[5] and many others. Such men as Edward Stanley of N.C., despise the meanness of such doings, too much, to allow them to be cold, when this subject is to be brought up.

Yours, very faithfully,

SAMIVEL WELLER, jr.

P. S. I hope the people mean to watch narrowly the course of Congress at the approaching session. Let them not forget that the *great contests of the session will relate to the admission of Florida and Texas to the Union*. Let all, or the most of their positions be made to bear on these points. Wake up the people, or all is lost.

SAMIVEL.

# *ALBANY WEEKLY PATRIOT,*

## April 27, 1843

### *(First of Two Dispatches)*

*"Sam Weller" delivers a catch-up report on nine escapes, razzing the slaveholders and sometimes including inside information that could only have come from the person escaping. An assistant postmaster general is mocked for having turned down an offer of $1,300 for a man who subsequently disappeared. A Georgetown enslaver is urged to send $150 in reward money to his formerly enslaved man, now in Toronto, in return for Weller's not revealing how he got the "scar on the left cheek-bone" listed in a runaway ad.*

Washington, D.C.

April 12, 1843

MR. PRINTER: Spring business has begun! As a preliminary to what is to come, I wish to present my respects to a few old neighbors and personal friends, whose *chattels* left so late in the fall, that, I presume, most of them failed to reach Canada. As they are now out of harm's way, I shall resume my letters.

(1.) First of all, I desire to congratulate my old friend and neighbor, JOHN HARVEY, of Georgetown, that he did *not* accept the $900 Hon. Mr. Holmes, M. C. from Charleston, S.C., offered him last summer, for *Frank Douglass*. Frank would have had a sorry chance of fleeing from a place so far towards the equator. The Under-ground Railroad took him on with ease, from the Capitol! If neighbor Harvey hasn't a heart of stone, let him send Frank's *family* after him, on pain of my exposing *some* of his *domestic* misdeeds!

(2.) HENRY CHASE thanks his Boss for robbing him of *only* $4,832,[1] in 38 years past!

(3.) MAJOR HOVEY, the amiable assistant P. M. General,[2] who has so strong a love for VALENTINE THORNTON, (bright fellow, that VAL.!) that he would not take the $1,300 John Lyons offered for him, must be delighted to know that Mr. Thornton wouldn't take twice as much for his rights as a British subject!

(4.) HENRY GRAY sends his best love to Madam ELIZA JOHNSON, of Baltimore, and says he, *perhaps*, might be induced to marry her, if she will learn to keep her temper! At present he prefers a single state!

(5.) JAMES BOWSER trusts that ROBERT HUNTER, ESQ., of Prince George's co., Md., will take lessons in *liberality*. He means to return and *put up that entry*, between the house and kitchen, in a month or two, *if* he don't forget it! CHARLES WARRICK also thanks him for *that pass* to Washington.

(6.) GEORGE BAILEY hopes TOM BERRY, of Prince George's co., will never forget how well *that garden seed came up*! He is much obliged to JOHN ALLEN for *not* catching him, because he couldn't!

(7.) JOHN MOORE wishes to say to Dr. P. WARFIELD, that he has paid him $10 per month, for eight years, *for nothing*; and don't mean to be so cheated again.

Could you, Mr. Patriot, have seen the "fine, placid countenance" of Charles Warrick, when he got into the Underground Railroad cars. You would not have wondered at his master's solicitude in his behalf.

(8.) JAMES BAKER concluded he was too "genteel" looking to remain a slave in Prince George's co., to R. W. Hunter. And MATILDA KETTLE wants you to tell Dr. Kearney, Surgeon in the U.S. Army, that *she* is of the same opinion! I forgot to mention that James Bowser thought his own wife was entitled to a better name than Sally Brooks, and therefore chose to take a tour to the Springs!

(9.) Mr. J. Y. YOUNG, of Georgetown, D.C., is requested to transmit to Wm. Hall, Toronto, Canada, that $150 he speaks of, as *part pay* for the "scar on the left cheek-bone," if he doesn't want me to expose the way he got it! I think I will copy Dr. Warfield's advertisement; it is so rich in details.

## $150 REWARD.

Ran away from the subscriber, residing in Georgetown, D.C., on the night of the 24th of October, negro man, John, who calls himself John More, about twenty-eight years of age, six feet high, very dark visaged, stammers somewhat occasionally, *reads and writes well, and is a good mathematician*; is a sagacious, shrewd fellow; *a professor of religion, and an occasional exhorter.* His clothes cannot be described, as he *furnished himself amply.*

P. WARFIELD

In my next, I shall invite attention to the doings of a *British* functionary.

Yours truly,

SAMIVEL WELLER, Jr.

NOTE.—When John Moore came to Albany, and we desired to get a place for him to tell his wrongs to his fellow-christians here, we could find *no church* that would open its doors. *Seven were refused!*

—ED. PATRIOT.

# *ALBANY WEEKLY PATRIOT,*

## April 27, 1843

### *(Second of Two Dispatches)*

*In this dispatch, Smallwood complains of a slaveholding British consul who might try to recover two people he had enslaved, now in Canada, by accusing them of a crime—taking the clothes they were wearing! He claims to have led the visiting Charles Dickens to see a slave trader's jail. He rattles off nine other enslavers and purports to pass on messages from the people they formerly enslaved. And he urges slaveholders to free and pay wages to their workers.*

Washington, D.C.

April 17, 1843

Mr. PRINTER:

Sometime ago you remember our friend, Lord Palmerston,[1] issued a circular, requiring all British consuls, in slaveholding countries, to cease to hold slaves. I very much wish that the attention of the British Government could be turned to some of their functionaries in this country.

[(1.)] There is John McTavish, Esq., the consul at Baltimore, Md., who married the slaves of Richard Caton, Esq., (with the incumbrance of his daughter, attached). He is a slaveholder, and no very gentle one, either, as his fugitive slaves have more than once testified. There was a *woman* who fled from his lash, last spring, a year since. And in the fall, John Miniski* a fine looking young man, who got tired of working for nothing,

*Both were forwarded to Canada. ED. PATRIOT.

for one of Queen Victoria's servants. A Scotchman and a Yankee make hard masters! Their own energy makes them exact as much labor *without any proper motive to industry*, as they are accustomed to see performed where labor is well paid for. Now, why is this Mr. Tavish to be permitted to trample on the requirements of his Sovereign? *Perhaps*, as a special favor to *his* aristocratic American relatives,[2] the "10th article" might be stretched,[3] so as to recover John and Elizabeth, under the plea of "felony," in wearing off *some clothes*, instead of fleeing *in puris naturalibus*![4]

(You never heard how I learned Latin, did you? One day Boz Dickens and I were walking down to see Williams' *Slave Pen*, right in front of the President's House.[5] Boz, after turning up his nose, in his very curious way, at the flag, on the Capitol, began to quote some Latin stuff about hypocrisy and republican despotism, as he said. And I thought I would learn it, to use *in cursing slavery with*! And it comes very convenient, sometimes, when I'm at a slave auction, or looking at a whipping, or visiting the slaves, in connection with our operations, to vent my feelings in a language the woman-whippers don't understand! A surly slave-catcher actually took off his hat to me, when I denounced him as a "*monstrum horrendum*." I suppose he thought me some great one!) Leaving Mr. Tavish I will pay a passing tribute to some other worthies.

(2.) There is Charles Carroll, of Howard District, Md., whose relative, "Sam Castle," desires to be remembered to him. He forgives him his countless stripes,[6] in view of the fact that the *last one* has been laid on.

(3.) Wm. Jones assures Mr. Crumpton Gantt, of Huntington, that his fame, as a tyrant, shall *not* be spread as widely as it deserves!

(4.) When I was last at Baltimore, I found my old friend Henry Hylon, mourning because he hadn't heard of his faithful Henry Lucas. But I *now* assure him that Henry is perfectly well and happy.

(5.) You remember the interest Reverdy Johnson, Esq., of Baltimore, took,[7] last winter, to help you out of the clutches of the slaveholding convention. Lewis Jackson says he is a very kind master, and that he never would have left him, if *Mrs.* Johnson had been blessed with an *angel's temper*! Slavery does make *women, who imbibe its spirit*, into very fiends!

(6.) Tom Berry, of Prince George's county, Md., renowned for his cruelty to his poor victims, can hardly expect John Allen to forgive him, at present; while the scars on his back remain so bright and fresh! Oh, he's a terrible tyrant!

(7.) The Widders *is* desperate! There is Widder Henrietta Dawson, who drove her faithful Isaac Johnson to flee. And Widder Ann Page, (quite another thing from the image of beauty, life and joy, Will Shakespeare imaged,[8] in the Merry Wives of Windsor,) of Cambridge, Md., who compelled James Wright to seek, in Canada, that home she denied to his patriotism, in this, his native land! Then Widder Eliza Jones must mourn that her "boy, Bennett," is no longer willing to work for nothing. And Mrs. Washington, of New Orleans, may cry her pretty eyes out! but she will never see her Chas. Williams again! He loved to travel; his organ of locality[9] was large; he had heard of Toronto, Canada, and wanted to visit it!

(8.) Wm. H. Edes, of Georgetown, who keeps the Feed Store, and would not let you have a horse, last summer, because you was a stranger, in pursuit of a lost child, may consider himself punished by the loss of William Martin.

(9.) Finally, I must condole, once more, with that much afflicted man, Notley Maddox. Just before cold weather, Washington Bell left him; and then, *old* Henson, his *last* male slave, a man of 55 years of age, had the cruelty to leave his "dear, old, grey-haired master, to die alone." Even his smart fop of a son couldn't catch the old fellow, though he went to Baltimore on purpose. I set by his side, in the cars, as he returned; and the way he *did swear*, was a caution to MEMBERS OF

CONGRESS! The old man has *hired* two white laborers, for his farm. Don't he regret, now, that he hadn't sense enough to emancipate *seven* as good men as Maryland holds, who had grown up with him and his children, and were used to the farm and his ways, and *hire* them? If old Notley has a spark of manliness about him, if he is not afraid his grey head will yet go down to the grave in sorrow, let him emancipate the three daughters of Henson, and the innocent children of the oldest girl, and so cease to be a slaveholder! I have much regard for Notley. I have known him long; and I pray that he may be led to do it.

Yours, in hatred of

Republican slavery,

SAMIVEL WELLER, JR.

# *ALBANY WEEKLY PATRIOT,*

## May 18, 1843

*Smallwood, or at least his alter ego, claims to have visited Connecticut, where a woman, raped by her enslaver's son and brought north by her enslaver, makes her escape. He also describes helping to freedom a woman from Bladensburg—Smallwood's hometown—who claims to have lost a child due to the actions of her enslaver's wife. He quotes a missive from his supposed nephew in Pittsburgh, who mentions an uncle in Cincinnati in the escape business. Smallwood has evidently decided to appoint as Weller relatives all of his allies in the underground railroad.*

New Haven, (Conn.)

May 15, 1843[1]

*Mr. Printer*:—Being so far North on business connected with the *forwarding trade*, I take the liberty to send you a brief letter. I have a tale of truth to tell, of a man who came originally from the "land of steady habits:" and that man's name is LEWIS. He does business in New Orleans, and owns a plantation not far from it. A few weeks since he came to New York in one of his own vessels, and thence came on a visit to this city. He brought a female slave with him. His abuse of her at the Hotel where he put up attracted the attention of the landlord, who checked it; and the true-hearted Irish servants advised her to leave the tyrant. They told her to follow the banks of the canal till she came to the river, (at Northampton,) and then to follow the river till she got to Vermont, where she would be safe. She left on Sunday night, April 30th, and *walked two nights and one day, without food*, except a little she begged at an Irish shantee.[2] (An Irishman, you know, will always divide his last potato with the poor.) She found friends at Southampton, Mass., who sent her on, in safety. Lewis threatened to sell her when he got back. He had been offered $1100 for her.

His son had *used* her, as slaves are commonly used, and she is now pregnant by him. I could tell you horrible tales of the licentiousness practised on this man's estate.

Four men followed the poor victim from New Haven as far as Southampton, showing an advertisement offering $200 reward for her; but the Northern jackals could not help the Southern wolf—(lion he cannot be; they have noble savageness about them, that disdains to oppress the weak.)

When I came on here, I took a poor abused creature from Bladensburg, who was held in slavery by George Taylor. She was once owned by John Orndoff, of Baltimore, a flour dealer, who failed, and sold her to Taylor. The wife of one of her several owners—no matter which—was in the habit of following Dr. HUN's advice,[3] and abused her. Rachel believes her little child was so injured by her mistress' unkindness, that she died. Poor Rachel! "She wept, and refused to be comforted," when she spoke of this lost one! I have often remarked to you that slavery makes women more brutal than men.

In connection with this, I wish you would print a part of a letter from my dear Nephew Joshua, at Pittsburgh. He says:

"You know the winter is not the season for us. Yet we have shipped four for the land of Victoria, three women and one man, all from Virginia. They came here after the lake navigation had closed and we had them on hand all winter, but they were not damaged. Now, if their Virginia masters knew how they came here, they would stare and they would swear, that we had not only an under-ground railroad, but an under ground steamboat navigation.

"The spring business has just commenced, and we hope we shall have a good run. A steamboat, from down south, came to this place last week, with a man on board called a slave—a thing; but this thing, strange as it may seem, stepped on shore, and took the under ground railroad for the land of *Victoria*. (Victory!) The master (so called) missed him, and streaked it for the Mayor's office, and took the high constable aside and offered him a large reward to apprehend the man; he thought he might use his legs this once for his own benefit; but the constable told him that he did not 'do such dirty work.' Told him, further, that he could get no one in Pittsburgh to do it for him, unless it was some outside piece of creation; and if any such could be found base enough to do such a thing, they would be mobbed and egged. He then applied to his honor, the Mayor, but had no better luck; so you see our location for business is a good one. This southerner may go home as Mr. Crooks had to do; it will not quit cost to hunt fugitives from injustice in our smoky city.

"We have not lost a cargo since we commenced. We have two or three ways to *Victory* from this point; so you need have no fears, and we hope you will not give Uncle all, and us none.

"I was down in Cincinnati, not long since, and found there another of our uncles, who is doing a large business, and the prospects of the rising reputation of our distinguished family was never as flattering as at present. We will stand much higher after this business of the season is over. I think we will have to have another life of the family writ, if we can find any body fit to do it.

"Your loving cousin,

"JOSHUA WELLER,

"Of the firm of J. Weller & Co.

"Pittsburgh, April 28, 1843."

JOSH is a sad fellow! True chip of the old block!

Yours for liberty,

SAMIVEL WELLER, Jr.

## *ALBANY WEEKLY PATRIOT,*

### June 15, 1843

*Smallwood gives "Sam Weller" an impressive title, as the agent of not just the underground railroad but all other means of escape as well. He records multiple escapes; boasts of daring to drive runaways past the offices of John Zell, a Baltimore constable; and wishes that Torrey ("Mr. Printer") could taste the spring peas served by Gadsby's Tavern in Alexandria, Virginia. And he brags about bribing police officers from the city's new Auxiliary Guard.*

### WASHINGTON CORRESPONDENCE.

Washington City

June 6, 1843

Mr. Printer,—Here I am, back to my post, as general agent of all the branches of the National Underground Railroad, Steam Packet, Canal and Foot-it Company.

Business begins to be very brisk. I have sent off no less than nine passengers, from this city, within a week! The most of them have taken the Erie Branch, Steam Flying Machine, so that you will not see them, or they you, unless the wind blows them very much out of their course. The nefarious attempt to swear a poor colored man, named Meade, of Baltimore, into prison, on pretense that he was in my employ, did not succeed, as you know. And the result of his acquittal has been to give a new impulse to business. Our agents *were* becoming a *little*, very little, too bold; and, while we were diverted to see the poor police officers, Zell, Ridgely and Hays, make such a blunder in their man, it seemed to show us the need of more boldness, which is the best caution. So the other day, when I took

Richard Brown to Baltimore, we went and laughed in their faces, as one of them was reading Waters' advertisement. Poor puppies! I have taken a *load*, at mid-day, right by their office, and the lazy dogs didn't look up! You remember JOHN WATERS' place, near the Columbia College,[1] on the road we often walked, when we were discussing the "affairs of the nation!" 'Tis a beautiful, shady spot. And Waters isn't *half* so bad as he might be!—But Dick,—I mean Mr. Richard Brown,—preferred Kingston, in Canada, where he has relatives, to all the charms of the Farm.

The day after he left, we passed along the *goods* of James Berry, who thought that Mr. JOSEPH CHAPMAN, of Norfolk, Va., had no better title to his services than Gray had to those of Latimer![2] Poor, benighted fellow! He had never read the convincing arguments of Rev. Mr. DEW,[3]—(alas! he could not read!)—so that it is not so much to be wondered at. So he took the new steamer to New York, and sent on his goods to my care. I learn that there is not much doing in the Human Cattle Market, of Norfolk, just now.—There have been but few sent to New Orleans, this spring, compared with former exports. Prices very low. The sensation caused by the Latimer case has not yet subsided. James' friend (my agent,) writes me that James and Latimer were old acquaintances; and Latimer will be glad to learn from you, of James' safety. [He is in Canada.—ED. PAT.]

On my return home from the North, I stopped a day or two in the upper part of Maryland. One result of my visit has been several indications of *powers of locomotion* never before exercised. Charles Smith thought he had toiled for THOMAS AYERS, of Hartford,[4] for nothing, quite long enough. Bill Dagin had the same view of his relations to WM. BELL, of the same place. Their masters are pretty clever fellows, a little fierce, at times, especially Bell. But liberty is sweet. David Colmon, of the same place, thought proper to leave WM. PITES; and Mr. HENRY GUIDON'S service had no charms for Stephen Hall, without pay! *Steve* is a queer fellow. The way he rolled up his eyes, half tearful, half mirthful, when he crossed the old Mason and Dixon's line, was funny!

Oh, how many scenes of deep interest I have witnessed, on that spot! Last year a large company were so affected that they embraced and kissed the stone that marks the line of Pennsylvania, weeping over it, and then shouting out for joy of heart!

Stephen Perkins wanted me to send his love to JAMES CHAMBERLAIN, of Easton. And his wife, Lydia, wished to be remembered to CHARLOTTE EVANSON, and to say, that not all the love she *might* have borne her as an equal *free* woman, could persuade her that it was right to suffer her unborn infant to become a slave to a woman not much whiter than its mother!

WATSON SWAN, of Baltimore, will not hereafter be troubled to distinguish his boy John Thomas, from other *white* young men, when he passes them in the street. Even according to Southern notions, Swan was doing a *black* deed, to enslave a worthy young man quite as white as himself. But my time is so occupied with the cares growing out of the great extension of my business, that I must postpone further notices of individuals, for the present.

The weather, here, is very warm; and the supply of vegetables in the market abundant. I wish I could send you some of Gadsby's green peas,[5] on which I luxuriated yesterday. Do come on and make us a visit, Mr. Printer!

By the way, the slaveholders this season, have advertised the fugitives but very little, in the political papers. They are trying them hard at handbills, and fees to the Auxiliary Guard and the Police. But we have *bought up* a few of the *Guard*, and you know we always despised the regular police as a set of poor tools!

Yours, respectfully,

SAMIVEL WELLER, JR.

# *ALBANY WEEKLY PATRIOT,*

## June 22, 1843

*Smallwood castigates an officer at the nearby Navy Yard for whipping an enslaved woman. He describes overhearing at Washington's city jail a plot to sell a free Black man by falsely claiming he is enslaved. This episode prompts him to complain of the atrocious treatment of free African Americans, particularly by policemen exploiting the 10:00 p.m. curfew for all Black people. He adds a sober passage analyzing racism and ends with an unusual sign-off: "Yours for* equal *rights."*

### WASHINGTON CORRESPONDENCE.

Washington, D.C.

June 14, 1843

MR. EDITOR:

I have various odds and ends to put together today—some old, some new.

I believe you remember the introduction I gave you, one day, to Capt. Pendegrass, of the Navy? He is a son-in-law of that fine old soldier, Com. Barron. But he is as unlike him, in every respect as possible. I have a rod for his back. He is from Pennsylvania, but he must needs ape the manners of the place, and hire a slave, in his family. So he hired one from one of the notorious C——s, of Maryland[1]—notorious for their severity to their slaves. She is a mother of three or four children, from whom she is separated, to wait on the wife and children of this Pennsylvanian. C—— told him "not to let her want for whipping." Accordingly, Mr. P. bares, as it were, the bones of the poor woman. Is he not a fine specimen of a Naval Commander? WOMAN-WHIPPING IN THE NAVY-YARD AT WASHINGTON! How would it sound in London, or Rome! Why, the arch Inquisitor would shake his sides for laughter, in scorn of these pretenders to republican freedom!

Let me advert once more to some slighter details. A few months ago, I went up to the old jail to witness the *sale of a woman at auction*, for debt. It did not take place, as the master concluded to pay his debt, and reclaim the victim.

While I was standing in the entry of the jail, a constable brought in a dark negro man—his face bruised and his clothes soiled—bearing very evident marks of the drunken loafer species; though he was sober enough at that time. He was a free boy, and not detected in the violation of any law. Why, then, was he imprisoned?

The jailor and constable talked the matter over, in my hearing, and their explanations amounted to this: He was committed to prison as a *runaway slave*. The constable, with a becoming wink and smile, added, "Why, if he don't turn out to be so, we must let him go, at the time."

Meanwhile, the fees of the constable, jailor, and District Marshall, (for maintenance,) are secure, from the Treasury of the United States! And as the freeman whose rights are trampled on is a friendless stranger, and one whose bad habits deprive him of public sympathy, no one is concerned to interfere.

This is a sample of the petty legal oppressions to which the free colored man is occasionally exposed in this city. The oppression under the 10 o'clock law, of the City Corporation, by which all free colored persons who are out later than that hour are liable to be arrested, put in the watch-house till morning, and then fined $5, or less, at the discretion of the Magistrates, I have often noticed. That the Corporation has no power to pass such a law, I need not stop to show.

In one instance, last fall, a servant of Daniel Webster's was thus dealt with; but Webster had no idea of submitting to the petty ordinance, and sent his lawyer, Mr. Hall, to contest its validity. The Magistrate thought it best to free the servant, without exacting the fine!

But with the colored man or woman who lacks so powerful a protector, the case is otherwise; and the lawless ordinance is sometimes enjoined with every circumstance of oppression.

An active City Magistrate told me to-day, that the enforcement depended very much on the *caprice* of the constables! If one of these worthies did not make quite so much as his pockets required, in the *more honorable* part of his duty, he would watch his chance to pounce on some helpless colored people that were out late, perhaps on their return from church, or a visit to their friends: and either put them in the lockup and have them fined, or let off for a private payment to the *constable*, of a *part of the fine*! That such barefaced highway robbery is perpetrated, I have no doubt. It is impossible for the colored man to prevent it, or get redress, as his color is a bar to his evidence against the white constable; and the laws of the United States, or city ordinances, that Congress sanctions by *not* revoking them, will bear the oppressor out in his iniquity.

The ordinance, it is true, was not generally enforced, *till reward was established*: but the very caprice in regard to its enforcement, made its action the more oppressive. No constable would think of enforcing it against any of the more wealthy and well-known people of color. So that those who are commonly the sufferers, are the most helpless of their class.—This is the true instinct of lawless power, to bind the heaviest burdens on those who are least able to bear it. It is the *meanness of slave holding chivalry.*

The same disposition is shown in the ordinary intercourse of white people with colored men and women, both bond and free. The *tone of command* is that which is almost always employed, in addressing them, no matter what the subject may be. To speak to them with respect, would be to *descend* to their level, in the view of the community. If the tones used are kind, they are still the indications of the kindness of an acknowledged superior, towards one accustomed to be treated as an inferior, for no other reason than their different color. The difference between the atmosphere of Washington, and one of our northern cities, in this respect, strikes the mind at once, and with great force. And there is a degree of timidity, and a want of self-respect, apparent in the manners of a large part of the people of color, which very naturally results from this state of things: and which would soon disappear, as it has in northern cities, under a different course of treatment.—There are exceptions, it is true, and marked ones; but just sufficient to confirm the general truth of what I have said.

Yours for *equal* rights,

SAMIVEL WELLER, JR.

# *ALBANY WEEKLY PATRIOT,*

## June 29, 1843

*Smallwood recounts two local cases of people kidnapped and enslaved, a serious threat to free African Americans even in the north. He remembers a just-deceased former aide to George Washington. And he again attacks the Auxiliary Guard police officers, whom he claims wait outside Black churches in order to extort fines or bribes from those who have stayed past the 10:00 p.m. curfew for African Americans, free or enslaved.*

### WASHINGTON CORRESPONDENCE.

### FREEMEN MADE SLAVES!—KIDNAPPING IN WASHINGTON!—MORE OF THE AUXILIARY GUARD!

Washington, D.C.

June 6, 1843

*Mr. Editor,*—I have some things of much interest to communicate, that I write again sooner than I anticipated.

Twelve years ago a Mrs. Hardy, of Maryland, died, leaving all her slaves, by her will, to her brother, Basil Hatten, with a provision that they, *with their increase*, should be free at his death. There was a farther provision that, if any were not of age, they should be put to trades—the males till they were 21, the females till they were 18.

Hatten died just about 12 years after his sister. The people, being now free, many of them removed to this city.

Mr. Robert Hunter, the heir-at-law, claims as his slaves, all the children who were born between Mrs. Hardy's death, and the death of her brother, notwithstanding the clause in the will to free the "increase!" He claims that they do not come under the provisions of the will; and that the "increase" refers to the children already born at the time Mrs. Hardy died.

Some of them were pretty well advanced, though not of age. But he made no provision for them, nor attempted in any way to control them, with one exception. He *fooled* one to remain with him on his plantation. The rest he could not deceive, so he cared nothing for them.

In order to carry out his designs against the children, he employed certain noted slave hunters in Maryland, to come to this city and kidnap them, which they did; six in number. They came on the SABBATH DAY, just about church time, that there might not be an uproar. They stole them, and carried them into Maryland. The case is now in law. The result is very uncertain.

This is not the only instance of kidnapping in Washington. I know a colored man named Henry Chub, who sometimes worked about the dock, loading and unloading vessels. He, with two of his sons, had been unloading a vessel, and after discharging her, he went ashore, leaving his sons to clear out the hold of the vessel. In the mean time the captain set sail, and carried off the two sons into slavery, to the unspeakable grief of their parents, who were both *free born*!

Similar acts have often been done, and are still doing, in this Metropolis of *free* and *christian* America; whose free institutions (!!) are so much admired; and who keep God's children in abject slavery, and utter ignorance, with as much boldness as if an express command from God sanctioned the atrocity! Do Americans think that the rest of the world have not sense enough to see and despise their hypocrisy?

I come now to notice the death of a Christian and Patriot, in the person of JOHN CAREY.[1] He died on the 2d ultimo, about 9 o'clock, P.M. No person, I presume, in this city, has enjoyed a greater degree of the confidence of the public on account of his *truly* CHRISTIAN EXAMPLE. He was a member of the First Baptist Church. The body was brought into the meeting house, on the Sabbath afternoon, attended by several clergymen. The Pastor, Rev. Obadiah Brown, delivered an excellent discourse. He stated that Carey was born in Westmoreland County, Va., in 1729, as he had learned from documents that he had recently seen. This made him 114 years old next August. Gen. Washington, who knew how to appreciate worth, in a black, as well as a white man, chose him for his body servant. He was with him in the old French war, at Braddock's defeat and throughout the revolution. He was often in the ranks, helping to fight the battles of his country. At the close of the war, Gen. Washington gave him one of his regimental coats, which he always wore, especially on public occasions.

And what reward did the *grateful Republic* give him for his services? Why, a few months before his death, by the exertions of Hon. GEORGE N. BRIGGS, of Pittsfield, Mass., Congress was induced to pass a bill giving him a pension, for the rest of his life. He received about enough to bury him decently! Most grateful country! Most magnanimous Congress!

I wish to bestow a passing notice on the AUXILIARY GUARD. Don't let the people forget these scoundrels! They have established a *new branch of business*;—it is, to station themselves in the streets, near the meeting houses of the colored people, and watch if any are later than 10 o'clock in returning home, to compel them to pay fines, if they are free, or else send them to the work-house. If they are slaves, their masters must pay, or they are whipped, for the CRIME *of attending on the public worship of* GOD, a few moments later than 10 o'clock! JOHN LITTLE and WILLIAM COX are very active in this business. Little is too lazy to support his family in any other way; and he is as famous for administering *discipline* to his wife! as he is for negro hunting! How long will the people of the North agree to support these scoundrels?

You remember my telling you, that in the recess of Congress, the colored people suffer much more than when Congress is here. It has been peculiarly so, since the last session. God help the poor, defenceless ones!

Yours, for liberty,

SAMIVEL WELLER, JR.

# *ALBANY WEEKLY PATRIOT*,

## August 22, 1843

*Smallwood corrects Torrey and tells the story of a man (described in two previous dispatches) who had escaped slavery but later returned to his enslaver. He renews his attack on the Auxiliary Guard, faulting northern members of Congress for funding the police unit. He notes a slowing of the domestic slave trade in Washington but complains that free Black residents of the capital are being detained in Maryland, if they don't have papers proving they are free, and sold into slavery.*

Washington, D.C.

June 11, 1843

MR. PRINTER,—I am sorry to say that you are wrong in regard to Mr. Martin's return.[1] He *did* come back to his master with a lie on his tongue in regard to the treatment he received from abolitionists. Happily he did not go by the underground railroad, so that he cannot interfere with our business at all. What he came back for; whether he was sent originally as a spy, or only meant to return to help off some of his relations, or whether he was too lazy to work among *freemen*, remains to be seen. The reflecting slaves are too intelligent, and have too much acquaintance with the friends of liberty, through their escaped relations, to be deceived by such a poor creature.

I have many things to say, some of them of thrilling interest. They stir even my old blood (for I am growing to be an old man, though I sign my name "jr." while the old man lives). I have before spoken of the rascally AUXILIARY GUARD, imposed upon the people of this city by northern Whig Representatives, for the support of which the people of the free States are heavily taxed. Its business appears to be nothing but *hunting the colored people*! You know it was argued in Congress that it was necessary to appoint this Guard to protect the private and public property. But the nearest they come to it is by their unceasing watchfulness over the *slave property*, and the free people of color, that they may exact fines and rewards out of them. Every one they can lay their hands upon, who is out after 10 o'clock at night, is fined five dollars and upwards, and if it is not paid has to go to the workhouse, if free, or be whipped if a slave. It is a fact that cannot be controverted, that since the appointment of this Guard there have been many more destructive fires and daring robberies than ever occurred at any period before, in the same length of time, and why is it so?—Because, while the guard are prowling about and hunting the colored people, there is nothing to hinder the misdeeds of robbers and house burners. I will give you an example of recent occurrence.

There has been a great revival of religion here, among both the white and colored people. The colored people being limited to 10 o'clock, and having, as you are well aware, no chance to hold meetings in the day time, except on the Sabbath, concluded one night to remain all night in the meeting house. As it was their own property they did not suppose any body would trouble them. But a little after 10 o'clock at night, while they were carrying on the meeting, the whole guard went in a body, and were about to take them all to the watch house, males and females, to keep them till morning. But they finally agreed to take their names only, if they would agree to come forward the next day and pay their fines. The colored people employed a lawyer to defend their cause, which is not yet decided.

Pray you, ask the good people of the North, whose Representatives established this guard, what harm were the colored people likely to do to "public or private property," by worshipping God, as Paul once did, till daybreak? And that too in their own house. Is not this atrocious act enough to show the character of the guard?

There have been very few colored people sold from the district this season, owing, I suppose, to the depreciation in the value of human chattels, or slave labor.—But some of the *free* citizens of the District have been sold in Maryland. Many of the proprietors of the landings on the Potomac get their hands from this District. On their return home, some of them come through Maryland, and if they happen not to have their free passes, they are seized, put in jail and sold. In the course of the last month, several from this city were reduced to slavery in this way. I know one poor fellow who made his escape and got home to Washington. They followed him here, took him, kept him in the slave-pen one night, and the next morning carried him in fetters back to Maryland. There was none found to rescue him! He is in Prince George's Co., adjoining the District.

You see that the constitution and laws of our country afford even the free man little protection against the tyranny of the slaveholders. When will the people of New York awake to see that they are our real oppressors? Why did your Mr. Barnard[2] vote for the ferocious "Guard," without thinking or caring for the inevitable use of it for the destruction of the social happiness of the unprotected people of this district?

I will try to write again to-morrow, for my paper is full, and I am called off to attend to *business*, and when business calls I must even leave my pen, which is a matter of regret when I can expose the knavery of the robbers and tyrants who rule this capital of the nation. I do love to see them snarl as I walk about the District, and note their wincing under my lashes. Would that every stripe I give came from the end of a *motive eleven feet long*,[3] wielded by the experienced hand of Josh Staple's, or his dirty scoundrel of a pen-keeper, Jones,[4] in hearty contempt for these white-livered knaves.

SAMIVEL WELLER, Jr.

# *ALBANY WEEKLY PATRIOT*,

## September 12, 1843

*Here Smallwood focuses on the domestic slave trade, which shipped the enslaved from the Chesapeake region to the booming cotton and sugar plantations of the deep south. He suggests that a tariff has gained support in the "breeding" states—the states in the upper south where babies born into slavery were valued mainly for the goal of eventually selling them south. He also describes sixty people marched past the Capitol in chains on their way to a ship that would take them to Louisiana. He faults the Whig Party for enabling the human trafficking.*

Washington, D.C.

September 12, 1843

DEAR PRINTER:

The devil is *not* dead, whatever reports may have been circulated to the contrary.

You know I am whig, in general, to the back bone! But that don't make me love all the evil deeds of that most wicked party.

They thought they had done a neat thing when they passed their last year's tariff. The sober, long-faced Yankees were told how it would "protect" their wool, and glass, and nail and shoe factories, and *forty* other things. And so, all your pious and benevolent people were full of delight at its passage. It would *help them to get rich*, faster!

What cared they for the anguish of broken hearts in *these* parts, if they could only make money? What cared they about the details of the system by which the *American slave trade was revived*? Why, their members, in Congress, voted for those very parts of the tariff on purpose to make the tariff popular in all the *breeding* states. And I have dropped into Jones' News Room, now and then, and seen these northern tariff papers copying articles from the organs of the Virginia and Carolina slave Traders and Breeders, in praise of the tariff, in proof of "a great change in public sentiment" at the South, in favor of the tariff! No doubt of it! I will tell you why, in a few words.

The new duties on *Sugar* have raised its price, all over the country. The price in New Orleans has been rising all the season. This has raised a new demand for slaves in the sugar country, and induced more to go into the cultivation. Hence the demand for slaves, in this, the Great National Slave Market, has been greatly increased.

Last year, not over 2,000 human cattle were sold in the shambles, in this city. This year, over 5,000 have already been sold at our dens of diabolism; and many more heart-strings will be broken before the winter sets in, by sundering all the ties of life, to meet the demand for human victims in the Louisiana market. In Florida, also, the demand has been greatly increased, by the diabolical *whig* law, to "encourage the armed settlement of" that slavery cursed Territory, and thus increase the political weight of the slave system in the councils of our country.

Scenes have taken place in Washington, this summer, that would make the devil blush, through the darkness of the pit, if he had been caught in them. Why, a fortnight ago, last Tuesday, no less than

SIXTY HUMAN BEINGS

were carried right by the *Capitol* yard, to the slave ship. The MEN were *chained* in couples, and fastened to a log chain, as is common in this region. The women walked by their side. The little children were carried along in wagons.

To make the shame and infamy of the Nation more perfect, it only needed the presence of some whig and democratic congressmen to shout "the *other* great interests," and so drown the sobs of the victims; and a *Chaplain* to pray over this every day sacrifice of the "patriarchal institution." One of the "proslavery ministers in the county of Madison," addressed in that noble letter of G. Smith's,[1] who are so afraid of having the *Sabbath Day* made the instrument of man's redemption from temporal and spiritual bondage, would be a very suitable person to officiate in that capacity.

Oh, your northern Christians may sanction and uphold all these atrocious deeds, by *their votes*; and it will "violate the Sabbath" to warn them to repent of such enormities, and break *their own vote-made yokes* from off their brothers' necks!

But I must stop, or I shall grow "imprudent;" a thing never charged on any of the *Weller* family; nor shall it be on

Your humble servant,

SAMIVEL WELLER, JR.

# *ALBANY WEEKLY PATRIOT,*

## October 24, 1843

*In the last of his Sam Weller dispatches—published ten days after Smallwood had arrived in Toronto with his family—he singles out for criticism the head of the Auxiliary Guard, Captain John Goddard, with whom Smallwood had recently had a run-in. He addresses Charles Torrey by his first name and complains about attempts to curtail travel north by African Americans. But he crows over the fact that his enemies "have not yet succeeded in discovering the underground railroad." Thus concludes Smallwood's writing for eight years, until his Narrative is published.*

### WELLER CORRESPONDENCE

Washington City

October 10, 1842 [*sic*, should be 1843]

DEAR CHARLES—I have a few things more to say about this region of oppression. Things are getting much worse here than they were a year or two past, or preceding the temporary reign of the Whig Congress; their measures, as regards the District of Columbia were mean and low, especially that auxiliary guard. You know that it is the legal business of every constable (according to the slave code, in Washington, as everywhere else in the South,) to hunt down colored people.—Well, you know that soon after the appointment of the famous auxiliary guard in Washington, by a Whig Congress, I noticed their negro-hunting in your excellent paper, which seemed to intimidate them some; but in order that they may accomplish their object of negro-hunting with more success and show of legality, they are *all* becoming constables; and among this number is the famous JOHN LITTLE, before noticed in your paper as one too lazy to support his family, but who did not spare the rod on his wife.

But again, another feature in the character of this guard is, that the Captain is no better than the rest. The Captain, Goddard,[1] has been appointed Magistrate, so that he might the better subserve the interest of the slaveholder here. I will give you a small specimen of the dirty work of this Captain and his guard, and then your Northern readers may be able to see how well that Whig Congress was employed, by which it was appointed; they may also see the mean and dirty acts of their Northern Representatives, in supporting such measures, and that they are no better, or not as good, as Southern slaveholders! There were two females on the 4th instant who started for Canada. On the day preceding their departure, this Goddard was seen loitering about the house in which the two females were, and at night he, with his guard and some of the regular police, (as they are termed,) encompassed the house, and with some of his lackeys entered, and demanded of each one his or her papers. The loafer Goddard said to them, "We understand you are going to Canada, and are going to take off some slaves with you." It so happened that there were several colored persons there, who came to see their friends off—among them were two slaves, a young woman and a young man. The woman, it appears, had come by the permission of her mistress; but without the knowledge of the woman, it was intended for a trap; for her master had disguised himself and employed the guard to follow her to the house where these females were, expecting that they were going to take her away with them. They carried her home, to see if her mistress had given her permission to leave the house.

The young man had a sister who was a member of one of the families, and was also going to leave with them. They took him away without letting him take leave of his sister—probably for the last time—in the midst of her tears and entreaties, though his master did not thank them for it; but it shows the part the Northern people have, through their Representatives, in oppressing colored people in this country; while they think to themselves that they have no sin of this kind to answer for; but they will be much mistaken—they will be like the Pharisees—"except ye repent ye shall likewise perish."

I shall close now. You perceive I have been brief; but I shall give you a full detail of everything going on here, in my line, as soon as I can, especially about the man who disguised himself, named Chas. Miller, near the Navy Yard.

Adieu, yours, &c.,

SAMIVEL WELLER, JR.

P. S. My dear nevvy Charles, I hope you will pardon me for adding a few more thoughts just now, which occur to me.—They are these: The poor miscreant slaveholders, and their supple jacks "the guard," have attempted to form a system entirely to obstruct immigration and to destroy our business. They have fixed things so now, since they discovered that soon all their slaves would leave them, that no colored person can get a passage by any railroad or other public conveyance till some *white* person has been before a magistrate and sworn that such colored person is free. This is the case both in Washington and Baltimore. Bah! did the poor man-thieves think this would have any tendency to check immigration Northward? The slave asks none of their modes of conveyance. Thank Heaven they have not yet succeeded in discovering the under-ground railroad, or to ☛ *blot out the north-star, or* DETHRONE GOD! all of which things they would do—☛ *if they could.* But aye, there's the rub—they can't do it!

A pretty state of things this, in the capital of a free government, whose constitution guarantees to all citizens, rights of citizenship everywhere in the Union!—But slaveholders violate the constitution, and nothing is said about it. Do you know the reason? It's because the North dares not oppose their masters of the South; that's all. But the Liberty party[2] will oppose them one of these days, when they get the government, and our hope, down South, is, that it will not be long before they will. At last the slaveholders begin to talk to themselves. By the way, they are thunderstruck at the results of the election in Indiana and Illinois! Good—let them quake, as well they may.

Remember me kindly and most heartily to all our dear friends, and especially to Uncle Slick.

S. W., Jr.

# A NARRATIVE OF THOMAS SMALLWOOD

# A NARRATIVE OF THOMAS SMALLWOOD, (COLOURED MAN:)

Giving an Account of His Birth—
The Period He Was Held in Slavery—
His Release—and Removal to Canada, etc.

Together with an Account of
the Underground Railroad.

Written by Himself.

TORONTO:
Printed for the Author by James Stephens,
5, City Buildings, King Street East.

1851.

## PREFACE.

We live in stirring times! perhaps in no period of the world's history, in the annals of no ancient clime, in no grand epoch of the past, have any strange events taken place to which the present century may not produce a loftier parallel; we may call back to remembrance those days that have gone to the winds, and glance our eyes over even to those far ages bordering on the flood, and traversing the long flight of centuries down we shall never find an ERA so replete with the wonderful as that in which we live, at this present. No! not when Semiramis[1] flourished in all the pomp and splendour of an universal Empress upon an Eastern throne. When the coronet of her fame encircled the Terrestrial sphere and her luminous sceptre lit up the world, illuminating her constellation of Empires. Not in the full blaze of Assyrian glory and strength, from Nimrod to Sardinapalus, extending over a period of nearly fifteen hundred years, have so many extraordinary events taken place as are concentred in the last half century. We live in an age of epochs—every year, every day, yea every moment, is an era within itself.

In reference to the question of Slavery, it may be reasonably supposed, that the Lord of light and life will not for ever slumber, he will not for ever see his children trodden down under the iron hoof of Southern despotism, yes! and I would declare, had I the power, with the voice of Stentor,[2] in the market place of a World's Metropolis, that the great Jehovah would prove himself a traitor to the sacred cause of truth and justice, did he for ever refuse to hear the cries of perishing millions! But hark!

"Jehovah thundering out of Zion,
Thron'd between the cherubim,"

JOHN MILTON.[3]

may yet rain fiery hail upon this wicked land, as he did of old upon the cities of the Plains.—Why are they oppressed? Napoleon Bonaparte says, that "all men are born equal—science and talent alone can make a difference;" and our most renowned Orators and Poets have sustained the assertion, and have ever been the champions of freedom. "In the sight of our law, the slave trader is a pirate and a felon, and in the sight of heaven an offender far beyond the ordinary depth of human guilt."—(Webster.)

How is it possible that they, the slaveholders, can lie in peace when "darkness is over the face of the earth," in the night time, alas!—

"Nature's sweet restorer, balmy sleep,"[4]

that which Dr. Johnson[5] calls

"The parenthesis of human woe,"

and the great poet of the "Night Thoughts,"

> "Sleep, great nature's second course,
> The balm of hurt minds,"

can have no pleasures for them; the fact is, they have no consciences, or if they are possessed of any, they are made of brass or of adamant, on which no insertion may be made; or else, like india rubber, they stretch to all intents and purposes.

"Talk not to me" (says Lord Brougham)[6] "of rights—talk not of the property of the planter in his slaves, I deny the right—I acknowledge not the property."

Look to the old climes of Europe, where, for centuries unknown to history, monarchy and its twin brother despotism have reared their stronghold, and we shall find slavery swept away even there, by almost all the rulers of all the kingdoms on that continent, occasioned more or less, no doubt, by "the flood of British freedom, which, to the open Sea of the world's praise, from dark antiquity hath flowed." (WILLIAM WORDSWORTH.) Such were the words of the sweet "Poet of the Lakes;" and such, furthermore, was the language of the great Law Orator of Ireland: "I speak in the spirit of British law, which makes liberty commensurate with, and inseparable from, British soil, which, proclaims even to the stranger and sojourner, the moment he sets foot on British earth, that the ground on which he treads, is holy and consecrated by the genius of universal emancipation." (JOHN PHILPOTT CURRAN.)

I do not wish that my solitary opinion concerning slavery should be forced upon mankind, no! this, worse than feudal despotism, has met with execrations from the most splendid spirits, that ever adorned the world, and from the treasure house of memory I bring them forth, like an archangelic host, rallying at the command of some mighty leader, on the ethereal plains,—but yet,

> "I would not have a slave to till my ground;
> To carry me; to fan me while I sleep,
> And tremble when I wake, for all the gold
> That sinews bought and sold, have ever earned:
> No! dear as freedom is, and in my heart's
> Just estimation, prized above all price,

I'd much rather be myself the slave
And wear the bonds, than fasten them on him."

WILLIAM COWPER.

Sleep well, thou "amiable Poet," under thy monument at Olney; although thou didst not live to grace with thy lifetime our day, tens of thousands of hearts beat with the warmest affection to thy memory, our eyes and the eyes of generations not yet conceived, down through countless ages, shall shed tears of gratitude at hearing thy blessed name,—dear evangelical Bard whose fame shall ever be,

"By seraphs writ with beams of heavenly light."

When shall some mighty genius arise to fling a standard of light over the United States: when their own flag shall no longer be a subject for declamatory orators and punning poets.

"UNITED STATES! your banner wears two emblems—one of fame;
Alas, the other that it bears reminds us of your shame:
The White Man's liberty, in types, stands blazing by your stars;
But what's the meaning of the stripes? they mean your Negroes' scars."

CAMPBELL.[7]

Long before I had purchased myself from my owner I had a desire to visit Canada, although I had often heard many strange and romantic stories

"Of that green land, cradled in the roar
Of western waves and wildernesses."

REVOLT OF ISLAM.[8]

And I had already made up my mind

"That a land of slaves shall ne'er be mine."

LORD BYRON.[9]

So I went on my pilgrimage, where in times past as at the present, many

> "A footstep was heard in the rustling brake,
> Where the cotton tree shadow'd the misty lake;
> And a murmuring voice, and a plunge from shore,
> And the slave was seen in the south no more."
>
> PROFESSOR LONGFELLOW.[10]

And finally arrived in Toronto, QUEEN CITY OF THE WEST, where all may well exclaim in the language of the Idolized Bard of the "land of the heather and bell:"

> "Wha sae base as be a slave
> Let him turn and flee."[11]
>
> ROBERT BURNS.

But, even here, I have met a prejudice equal to any thing I ever experienced in the south. Thanks to the laws, it may go no further than verbal illustration! But the greatest prejudice of all is that against myself personally, held by people of my own colour, concerning that which they never had a chance of knowing the truth of, but which I have explained in the following pages to the satisfaction, I hope, of all enlightened and conscientious men.

It was to clear up my character, and do justice to humanity, that I was at first prompted to publish this pamphlet—for I was well aware that

> "Slander lives upon succession,
> For ever housed where it once gets possession."
>
> SHAKESPEARE'S *Comedy of Errors.*

And armed in the adamantine armour of conscious innocence and truth, I hope to repel the thrusts of

> "Slander
> Whose edge is sharper than the sword,

Whose tongue outvenoms all the worms of Nile."

CYMBELINE.

But it has been the lot of great men to be slandered. Clarkson and Wilberforce,[12] who ranked high among the truly great and good of the world, in their day, were slandered; but time and the good sense of mankind are doing these illustrious philanthropists justice; and so they will George Thompson,[13] who was so recently assailed by the tongue of slander in our city, whilst ably and disinterestedly engaged in protesting against the wrongs inflicted upon my oppressed and injured African brethren, now held in bondage in the so-called "LAND OF LIBERTY!"

## ADDRESS TO GEO. THOMPSON,[14] ESQ., MEMBER OF THE IMPERIAL PARLIAMENT.

"His life was gentle, and the elements so mixed in him, that NATURE might stand up and say to all the world—THIS WAS A MAN".

*Julius Cæsar.*[15]

LONG ages, may thy voice be sent
In anthems, loud and free,
From continent to continent;
Across from sea to sea.

Millions of hearts adore thy worth,
Yea, many nations bless
Thy name, renown'd through all the earth
As in this wilderness.

Advance with splendour and prevail
In thy triumphant course;

And distant ages yet may hail
Thee! second Wilberforce.

Still may thy mighty eloquence
Sweep on like western waves
Till opposition's banish'd, hence,
And freedom crown the slaves.

Long may'st thou stay to make us blest;
Display thy native charme:
Toronto, Queen of (all) the West,
Will clasp thee in her arms.

We love thee, in our hearts and souls,
For all thy virtues rare;
And while Ontario's water rolls
Thou shalt be mirror'd there.

This little work, with the exception of the quotations and a portion of the matter in the preface, is wholly original, containing a simple narrative of unvarnished facts, interspersed with such comments as I conceived to be necessary. I am led to make these remarks from the fact that I have seen a book for sale in this city purporting to be a production of Mr. Paola Brown, of Hamilton;[16] but the fact is, it is a copy, almost verbatim, of a book known as "Walker's Appeal," written by a coloured man of that name. And in order to shew the reader more plainly the diabolical attempt of P. Brown to rob the memory of an estimable man, of one of the boldest productions against slavery ever written and published in America, I will give the preface to a brief sketch of the life and character of DAVID WALKER; together with the sketch itself, written by Henry Highland Garnet, and published with the second edition of the book referred to in 1848. Hence it will be seen that Mr. Brown is not honest in putting forth a work like the one in question in his name and as his own production.

## GARNET'S PREFACE TO WALKER'S APPEAL

"Such is the very high esteem which is entertained for the memory of DAVID WALKER., and so general is the desire to preserve his 'Appeal,' that the subscriber has undertaken, and performed the task of re-publication, with a brief notice of his life, having procured permission from his widow, Mrs. Dewson.

The work is valuable, because it was among the first, and was actually the boldest and most direct appeal in behalf of freedom, which was made in the early part of the Anti-Slavery Reformation. When the history of the emancipation of the bondmen of America shall be written, whatever name shall be placed first on the list of heroes, that of the author of the Appeal will not be second.

Troy, N. Y., April 12, 1848.

## GARNET'S SKETCH OF THE LIFE AND CHARACTER OF DAVID WALKER.

"IT is generally the desire of the reader of any intellectual production, to know something of the character and the life of the author. The character of David Walker is indicated in his writings. In regard to his life, but a few materials can be gathered; but what is known of him, furnishes proof to the opinion which the friends of man have formed of him—that he possessed a noble and a courageous spirit, and that he was ardently attached to the cause of liberty.

Mr. Walker was born in Wilmington, North Carolina, Sept. 28, 1795. His mother was a free woman, and his father was a slave. His innate hatred to slavery was very early developed. When yet a boy, he declared that the slaveholding South was not the place for him. His soul became so indignant at the wrongs which his father and his kindred bore, that he determined to find some portion of his country where he would see less to harrow up his soul. Said he, 'If I remain in this bloody land, I will not live long. As true as God reigns, I will be avenged for the sorrow which my people have suffered. This is not the place for me—no, no. I must leave this part of the country. It will be a great trial for me to live on the same soil where so many men are in slavery; certainly I cannot remain where I must hear their chains continually, and where I must encounter the insults of their hypocritical enslavers. Go I must.'

The youthful Walker embraced his mother and received a mother's blessings, and turned his back upon North Carolina. His father died a few months before his birth; and it is a remarkable coincidence, that the son of the subject of this Memoir was a posthumous child.

After leaving home, David Walker travelled rapidly towards the North, shaking off the dust of his feet, and breathing curses upon the system of human slavery, America's darling institution. As might be expected, he met with trials during his journey; and at last he reached Boston, Mass., where he took up his permanent residence. There he applied himself to study and soon learned to read and write, in order that he might contribute something to the cause of humanity. Mr. Walker, like most of reformers, was a poor man—he lived poor, and died poor.

In 1827 he entered into the clothing business in Brattle street in which he prospered; and had it not been for his great liberality and hospitality, he would have became wealthy. In 1828, he married Miss Eliza ——. He was emphatically a self-made man, and he spent all his leisure moments in the cultivation of his mind. Before the Anti-Slavery Reformation had assumed a form, he was ardently engaged in the work. His hands were always open to contribute to the wants of the fugitive. His house was the shelter and the home of the poor and needy. Mr. Walker is known principally by his "APPEAL," but it was in his private walks, and by his unceasing labours in the cause of freedom, that he has made his memory sacred.

With an overflowing heart, he published his "APPEAL" in 1829. This little book produced more commotion among slaveholders that any volume of its size that was ever issued from an American press. They saw that it was a bold attack upon their idolatry, and that too by a black man who once lived among them. It was merely a smooth stone which this David took up, yet it terrified a host of Goliaths. When the fame of this book reached the South, the poor, cowardly, pusillanimous tyrants, grew pale behind their cotton bags, and armed themselves to the teeth. They set watches to look after their happy and contented slaves. The Governor of GEORGIA wrote to the Hon. Harrison Grey Otis, the Mayor of Boston, requesting him to suppress the Appeal. His Honor replied to the Southern Censor, that he had no power or disposition to hinder Mr. Walker from pursuing a lawful course in the utterance of his thoughts. A company of Georgia men then bound themselves by an oath, that they would eat as little as possible until they had killed the youthful author. They also offered a reward of a thousand dollars for his head, and ten times as much for the live Walker.

His consort, with the solicitude of an affectionate wife, together with some friends, advised him to go to Canada, lest he should be abducted. Walker said that he had nothing to fear from such a pack of coward blood-hounds; but if he did go, he would hurl back such thunder across the great lakes, that would cause them to tremble in their strong holds. Said he, 'I will stand my ground. Somebody must die in this cause. I may be doomed to the stake and the fire, or to the scaffold tree, but it is not in me to falter if I can promote the work of emancipation.' He did not leave the country, but was soon laid in the grave. It was the opinion of many that he was hurried out of life by the means of poison, but whether this was the case or not, the writer is not prepared to affirm.

He had many enemies, and not a few were his brethren whose cause he espoused. They said that he went too far, and was making trouble. So the Jews spoke of Moses. They valued the flesh-pots of Egypt more than the milk and honey of Canaan. He died 1830 in Bridge street, at the hopeful and enthusiastic age of 34 years. His ruling passion blazed up in the hour of death, and threw an indescribable grandeur over the last dark scene. The heroic young man passed away without a struggle, and a few weeping friends

'Saw in death his eyelids close,[17]
Calmly, as to a night's repose,
Like flowers at set of sun.'

The personal appearance of Mr. Walker was prepossessing, being six feet in height, slender and well proportioned. His hair was loose, and his complexion was dark. His son, the only child he left, is now 18 years of age, and is said to resemble his father; he now resides at Charlestown, Mass., with his mother, Mrs. Dewson. Mr. Walker was a faithful member of the Methodist Church at Boston, whose pastor is the venerable father Snowden.

The reader thus has a brief notice of the life and character of David Walker."

* * *

Let no one suppose that I have written this for the sake of pecuniary gain, such is not the case; but to defend myself against those who are not just enough to "render unto Cesar the things which are Cesar's." I have laboured night and day at my calling, therefore I have no need of charity at the hands of any one. And from the proceeds of honest toil I have given away many pounds. Six pounds would not refund what I have given to fugitives during the last fall and winter;—this I am prepared to prove.[18]

THE AUTHOR.

Toronto, July, 1851.

# A NARRATIVE OF THOMAS SMALLWOOD.

I was born in Prince George's County, Maryland, the 22nd day of Feb., 1801. I was recorded to be set free at the age of thirty, in the clerk's office of that county.[19] He who was instrumental in bringing it about was the Rev. J. B. Ferguson.[20] Myself and Sister had been bequeathed to the Lady whom he married and to her children. Although by the terms of the will he could not dispose of us, at pleasure, yet by paying the amount at which we were valued he could do so by mutual agreement with those interested. That he did (for he was no friend to slavery) by paying $500 for me, but with the amount he paid for my sister I never became acquainted. However I served until I was thirty years of age, and my sister until she was twenty-five, so as to work out what he had paid for us.

It is needless for me to go into a detail of the vicissitudes through which I passed during that period, more than to say, about five years before the time I was to be freed I hired myself from my master for the sum of $60 per year; about a year from that time I married.[21] From then to the expiration of my servitude it was more than the joint labours of myself and wife could accomplish to pay my hire and to support ourselves and children, hence it left me in debt at the end of my service $60, which I subsequently paid to the last farthing.

What little I know of the letter was obtained in the following manner, for I never had a day's schooling. The gentleman before mentioned, as my master, and his wife, learned me the English alphabet, and to spell in two syllables. When that became known to his neighbours they were amazed at the fact that a black or coloured person could learn the Alphabet, yea, learn to spell in two syllables. I appeared to be a walking curiosity in the village where I then lived,[22] and when passing about the village I would be called into houses, and the neighbours collected around to hear me say the Alphabet and to spell baker and cider, to their great surprise, (which were the first two words in the two syllables of Webster's Spelling Book.)

This may afford the reader a glimpse into the abyss of intellectual darkness into which the African race in America has been so long purposely confined, to serve the avarice and ends of their tyrannical oppressors, and to get out of which, by the aid of their friends, they are now struggling against many obstacles; prejudice on the part of the whites being among the most potent. But for my advancement from two syllables to the little I now possess I owe a deep debt of gratitude to a family of that people who are proverbial for their love of learning and imparting it to others, viz. Mr. John McLeod[23] a Scotch gentleman in whose excellent family I lived several years as servant. He had a large family of sons and daughters, these young gentlemen and ladies not only took great pleasure in learning me, but all the other servants about the house, who would take their teaching, for they were all coloured, and hired help notwithstanding.

He employed many servants about his house, he hired all; for be it said to his credit and humanity, he would own no slaves, although living in a slaveholding country.

I have ever declined the many opportunities and offers I have had to become a tool in the hands of the enemies of that class of people with whom I am identified, and these, without regret on my part, deprived me of a considerable portion of this world's wealth. If my memory be not at fault, I was from the year 1822 or 23, up to about 1830, an advocate of African Colonisation, because I thought the object of that Society[24] was the entire abolition of slavery in the United States; and which I thought would lead to its final extinction every where else. Thus placing my race, together with all others, in an elevated position.

But I was grievously deceived. The object and policy of that Society proved to be, under the mask of philanthropy, the draining off the free coloured population from among the slave population by inducing them to emigrate to Africa; for the doctrine of its leaders was that the free population contaminated the slave population with a spirit of freedom, which made them uneasy in their bonds, and made it very difficult for their oppressors to hold them. But said they, if we can get rid of the free negro population we can put a stop to any further emancipations, and thus have perpetual slavery without danger.

This they sought to accomplish by various modes,—one or two I will note. First, by the influence of the African Colonisationists it was decreed that no free coloured persons should be employed on any of the government works, in the United States, while, at the same time, they invited foreign emigration to supply their places. Thus, as much as possible, depriving them of a means of subsistence, in order to make them an easy prey to the wicked and insidious designs of the African Colonisation Society. Secondly, they had recourse to such of the coloured men who had acquired some influence over the minds of the free coloured people, among whom they lived, by holding out to them pecuniary inducements as a reward for their services in persuading and deluding their brethren into the African Colonisation trap.

My humble self happened to be among the number to whom inducements were held out. And for the sake of my influence in that direction, I could have become a merchant in the Liberia trade, backed with the aid and influence of that Society. But I preferred to live in indigent circumstances, and enjoy my morsel with a good conscience, rather than be possessed with wealth and a burning conscience, with a recollection that I had come into possession of these through treachery to my afflicted race.

The Slaveholders, themselves, can bear record that their gold and silver could not bribe me into a crusade against the interest of my brethren, and that while among them I bore an interminable hatred of their doings to them, and that I could not smother it, or else they would not have strove to entrap me as they did, and especially in 1843. I remember several occasions wherein I was concerned in secreting lots of fugitives who had been sold to the traders and fled to me that I might effect their escape, and the united rewards for whom, while I thus had them secreted, amounted from two hundred to two hundred and fifty pounds.

These facts are so notorious that it is no hard matter for me to prove them in this City. But there were not found wanting those of my coloured brethren, who became willing tools for the Colonisation Society, and among those who became so, and grew rich by it, was James Brown, and a Mr. McGill,[25] the former had been a particular friend of mine, but in consequence of his connexion with that Society we became opposed to each other and thus ended our friendship.

My feeble efforts in the meantime were devoted to the anti-slavery cause, but the difficult question with me was what could I do to help to push forward so good a cause. I knew that I was in the midst of a slaveholding community, in which, even the white man, who had more liberty and freedom of speech than I, dare not raise his voice in favour of freedom for the African's descendants in Christian America, although he might raise it as high as he pleased for the Greeks and Poles. I knew I could not go about the country and lecture against slavery, and that I could not call meetings to raise funds to help the poor way-worn fugitive toward the north star, seeking freedom from democratic and Christian Slavery.

However, I determined to do something in the matter, therefore I directed my efforts, first, against the influence of the Colonisation Society, among coloured people, and by the assistance of the Lord I was in them successful, for where I lived, not one in a hundred could be induced to go to Africa. And so it was when I left; but how it is there now I cannot tell, for since the passage of the fugitive law, the Colonisationists are moving heaven and earth as it were to induce the free coloured people of the states to emigrate to Africa.

The success of the fugitive bill may be attributed mainly to the influence of Northern Colonisationists, for any one having any knowledge of that fraternity cannot but have observed that it is composed mostly of the great merchants, manufacturers, and aristocrats of the North, who suck their riches from the

South off from the sweat and blood of the African race, with as little reason and humanity as the stall-fed hog sucks the swill that is poured into his manger. These are they who lauded the Idol of Massachusetts, Daniel Webster, the great apostate,[26] for the part he had taken in that infamous measure.

Secondly, to assist in the escape of all I could from Slavery, and after a time they crowded upon me by scores, and thank the Lord I was enabled to effect the escape of all except seven, who, through their own indiscretion and the treachery of others I was foiled in effecting their escape. It is extremely hazardous to undertake to do any thing for the slaves, but I do not blame them; it is just the way they are tutored in their raising. It is one of the grand policies of the slaveholders to keep up a continual lack of confidence on the part of the coloured people toward each other, whether they be free or bond, by inspiring them with jealousy and envy against each other in order to keep down that sympathy and mutuality which is so necessary among people having a common interest at stake. Finally, it is the slaveholders' policy to keep their slaves in ignorance of every thing except to know how to do their work and to act treacherously with each other; he or she that is the most expert at these, knowing nothing else, is, according to their language, the best negro.

Hence it may be easily seen that the task of doing for them is a most dangerous one. Therefore much could not be done in the way of the underground railroad* until 1842, at that time, that most excellent and whole-souled Abolitionist, the Rev. C. T. Torrey, made his appearance in Washington.[27] I had heard of his arrest and trial at Annapolis, the seat of the Maryland government, to which place he had gone to take notes of the proceedings of the slaveholders then assembled in convention, at that City, and I myself watched its progress with great anxiety. Although I was not at that time personally acquainted

*The origin of this technicality, *underground railroad*, is supposed to be this,—a number of slaves would sometimes disappear from a neighbourhood in the course of a single night of whom no trace could be obtained until they were entirely out of the reach of their astonished owners, which led them to exclaim, that, "the Negroes had a railroad under the ground."

with him, yet immediately after his acquittal and return to Washington, the seat of the government of that Union, I formed an acquaintance, with him through the agency of my wife, who took washing out of the house in which he then boarded; through her, I sought and obtained an interview with him.

And be it spoken to the praise of the lady with whom he boarded,[28] that she and my wife were the only assistance we had for some time in the execution of our plans. At our first interview he informed me of a scheme he had in view, and requested my assistance, to which I readily assented. The scheme had for its object the rescue of a family of slaves, consisting of a man, his wife, and several children, who were owned by Mr. Badger of North Carolina, a Cabinet Minister,[29] then living at Washington, and whose price for them was fifteen hundred dollars.

I was dispatched to see the woman and apprise her of the scheme, her husband being away North at the time begging money to pay for them. That good man thought that Mr. Badger had already got more of their labour than he was justly entitled to, according to the law of God; he therefore resolved if possible to deprive him of any pecuniary consideration for their liberty, in addition to the value of the labour he had already robbed them of. Besides, he was not in favour of paying slaveholders for any of their slaves that could be otherwise rescued from their grasp.

This the slaveholders and their proslavery apologists, yea, some who profess to look upon slavery with abhorrence, conceive to be monstrous, that the slaveholder should be deprived of his slaves without pay.[30] Even the Patriot of this City,[31] of the 4th of April, 1851, holds the following language in reference to it, "be thou just before you are generous." But they should also remember that justice has two sides, or in other words, a black side as well as a white side. And if it is just for slaveholders to compel men and women to work for them without pay, because they are black, and they have the power to do so; then it is equally just for them, or their friends, to deprive their masters of such labour without pay.

Besides, the slaveholders are the aggressors. The African race never sold themselves to any one, but they were stolen, and those who hold them in bondage are either the thieves or receivers, the one class being no better than the other and therefore the both are robbers. In common merchandise, if any are found with stolen goods in their possession, let them have come in possession of them ever so honestly, on their part, yet are they deprived of such goods without a return of any part of the price that they paid for them; and if they cannot give a good account how they came by them, they are punished as the principal thief. And if a thief be taken with the spoil in his possession, it is rescued from him, and he punished according to law.

Now the slaveholders and dealers are robbers both of God and men: first, according to their own language, "all men are born free and equal, and are endued by their creator with certain unalienable rights, among which are life, liberty, and the pursuit of happiness." Now the slave dealers and holders have robbed those they hold as slaves of those rights, and thereby robbed them of the happiness and pleasures flowing from the enjoyment of those rights. They have robbed God of that homage and praise due to him from beings with whom he has deposited those rights. They have robbed the world of the benefit of the intellectual part that God designed they should perform in creation. The Algerines used to take the subjects of other nations and make slaves of them, and demand a price for their freedom; some of the nations thus aggrieved gave them unmistakable proof that they would not submit to such injustice by sending against them some of their war ships to chastise them, and so put an end to it. So then, they who rescue those from the grasp of those who are continually robbing them are only performing the part of the good Samaritan, let slaveholders and their apologists say what they will.

However the man owned by Mr. Badger, rejected (or was induced to do so through the influence of Colonisationists, and others in the North, who are always very anxious to recognise and acknowledge a right of property by man in man) the proposition of Mr. Torrey and so begged the money and paid for his family. If that money had been placed in the hands of Mr. Torrey, he not only would have rescued that family but scores of others, who had as much claim on their misguided charity as that family had.

But this is only a small exhibition of their misdirected charity. I expected better things of Abolitionists, while I expected no good of Colonisationists. Notwithstanding these parties, without a murmur, would give their thousands to purchase a few individuals, they would complain bitterly against Mr. Torrey and myself if they were called upon by us to give a few shillings to those fugitives whom we sent among them, to help them out of harm's way. And frequently some of those gangs charge us with taking an undue amount of money from them, and this brings me to notice the mode of our operations.[32]

Its foundation was that we had two places of deposit between Washington and Mason's and Dixon's line. The distance between Washington and the first was thirty-seven miles, the second was forty miles from the first; over these our passengers generally travelled in two nights, and the third night they cross the line, and accomplish a distance of nine miles into Pennsylvania, to another place of deposit. And now I proceed to place the reader in possession of the mode of travel, on the so-called underground railroad. If we had women and children to convey, we had to hire conveyances at the rate of from fifteen to fifty dollars to the first place of deposit; the prices varied according to the numbers we had to convey. We had to pay teamsters a very high price in order to induce them to risk themselves and teams in so dangerous an enterprise. Besides, there was great difficulty in meeting with teamsters to whom we could make propositions of that kind. We have paid for the conveyance of one person fifteen dollars, for the conveyance of three twenty-five, and for eight or nine fifty dollars, for a distance of only thirty-seven miles.

I will relate one circumstance which took place during our operations which will serve to show how much justice there is in those charges before mentioned. About the latter part of August, 1842, the beloved friend, Torrey, who is now no more, was about to leave Washington for the North, and I desired he would take with him about fifteen persons,—men, women, and children; but how that could be accomplished was a question of considerable importance, it was next to impossibility to get a teamster to convey them at any price. So the only alternative left was to purchase a conveyance; and, then again, there was another obstacle in the way, almost insurmountable, which was the want of money, however I got over this by the aid of a confidential friend who acted with me in all confidential matters relating to our operations, for though we had great difficulties to contend with, yet there were many things that worked in our favour. There happened to be a huckster who had a wagon for sale that just suited our purpose, and for which he asked fifty-three dollars; the bargain was closed by paying the money.

The next point of difficulty which lay in the way was to obtain a span of horses; this, however, was got over by our calling on a teamster to whom we had given fifty dollars for one of those trips before alluded to, and who had a span for sale; although not very good, they answered our purpose. We therefore agreed to give him sixty-five dollars for them, paying twenty-five dollars down and I and my friend becoming responsible for the balance, which was forty dollars.

Those obstructions were now overcome, yet still there were others in the way, though not quite so potent. We had to get a set of harness, and a pole made for the wagon, all which was to be done in one day, for until the morning of the day preceding the night on which friend Torrey was to start with the fifteen, we had strove to hire a conveyance, but could not succeed, notwithstanding those persons had all been notified to meet at a certain place on that night, which notice could not be revoked, therefore the people were on the spot at the appointed time.

But we were not ready, therefore we had to conceal them in various places in the City; in the meantime morning arrived, and with it a terrible uproar. One had no one to get breakfast, Ann had absconded taking with her all her children; another had no one to black the boots, to set the table, and to wait breakfast, Bill had taken French leave, and gone about his business; and a third, had no one to drive the coach to church; others were also in as bad a fix, hence a general pursuit was instituted on all the roads leading North, but all to no purpose, for the people were yet in the City.

One man, by name Gunnell,[33] had a woman and two children whose husband desired to purchase them and for that purpose employed a gentleman to negotiate for them; but Gunnell insulted the gentlemen while he was trying to bargain for them, so he would have no more to do with the matter. The only alternative then left for the husband was to seek deliverance by flight, and for that purpose he with another man called on me to see what I could do for him in the matter; after telling his story and stating to me the various difficulties he thought I would have to contend with which to me was a mere moonshine except the getting of a little girl, between five and six years of age; that child was required to set all night by the side of a cradle in its master's and mistress' bed chamber, in order that if their child should awake, she should rock it, to prevent it from disturbing their slumbers. To get that child was the work of its mother, and to do it required some skill and caution. However, she did it admirably; it seemed, as if by special providence of the Lord, a heavy sleep had come upon her master and mistress so that she went into their bed chamber as she informed me since and took her child from the side of the cradle, without a stir on their part, never to be placed there again, to spend a weary night for their comfort, for she with her children arrived safe in Canada, and she is now in Toronto.

The husband of the woman told me that his wife's master frequently boasted that a neger could not beat his time; I told him that if he would perform the part I had given him to do, by the assistance of the Lord, I would beat his time, though a neger, according to his sense of the word. Thank the Lord, I did beat his time, and by the assistance of the Lord always could beat his and any of the rest of the slaveholders' time, but for the treachery of some of my own colour. He was on the six o'clock train of cars, the next morning, for the North, and his satellites on every road leading North. He went as far as Baltimore but returned again on the evening train of the same day, not having got the least tidings of them, and no wonder for they had not left the City.

But the beloved Torrey started that same evening after the setting of the sun with fifteen persons, men, women, and children, for the North. And here I must notice the remarkable interposition of the Lord in preserving them from capture; first, if we could have got ready they would have started the first night mentioned and the early pursuit which was made after them would have resulted in their capture; but, on the contrary, notwithstanding our untiring perseverance we could not get ready; the result was their pursuers had gone a day ahead; and when they were going, some of their pursuers were returning on the same road, and but for another fortunate accident which happened they would have been met on the road and captured by them; but just as they came to a thick bush, within a convenient distance of the first place of deposit, the wagon, without exhibiting any previous weakness whatever, suddenly gave way and they had to turn aside into the bush: while they were thus snugly secreted in the bush those who were hunting them passed by without seeing or hearing any thing of them, this also served as an excellent delusion and put an end to all pursuit in that direction, for it was concluded they had gone by water.

Mr. Torrey then went to our first place of deposit, procured another wagon, and proceeded North with the people until he arrived at Troy, N. Y., without their owners hearing any thing of them. I received a letter from him dated at that place containing these words in substance, "I have arrived at Troy safe, with the chattels, and am now shipping them on board of a canal boat for Canada, and then I shall leave for Lynn, Mass."

That feat having been accomplished, more satisfactorily to us than to the slaveholders, I turned my attention to laying plans for the performance of another; that I accomplished in some three or four weeks after, by sending off twelve or thirteen slaves, to the great annoyance of the slaveholders; notwithstanding there was a terrible uproar about that place, and a reward of two thousand dollars offered for the detection of the person or persons who were thus depriving them of their goods and chattels. But I continued to defy detection, and sent them off in gangs; never less than a dozen. I frequently had lots of slaves concealed about in Washington, who had fled to me for safety when they got wind that their masters were about to sell them to the slave traders, and when the united rewards for them would amount to from six to eight hundred, and a thousand dollars.

These then were the times if I was a traitor to my brethren,[34] with which my enemies have attempted to brand me, when I could have made my jack. But it is passing strange, and not be credited by any reasonable, just, and unprejudiced person, that I should for a paltry sum of a few dollars or pounds become an enemy to my brethren for whom I have almost worn myself out, while those who have had the audacity to accuse me, (who have stood in the midst of dangers for my race, beset on every side by enemies,) stand off at a respectful distance, out of harm's way, and like cowardly curs bark at slaveholders, but do nothing more. But on the contrary, I employed persons and furnished them with the means to purchase food for them until a convenient time should arrive for their departure, and then I would pack them off.

For several reasons the entire arrangement, management and setting off those gangs forward, I had to attend to myself, but it was not practicable for me to travel with them always, because suspicion had already pointed to me, and I could not be absent from Washington without its being known; therefore my absence at the times of the departure of those gangs might have led to my arrest, and an investigation, resulted in my conviction. Besides, I was the sole proprietor of the so-called underground railroad in that section, it having been started without the assistance of any earthly being save Torrey, myself, my wife, and the Lady with whom he boarded. Torrey having gone North the burden and responsibility of consequences rested entirely on me, therefore I had to watch every moment as with an eagle's eye. I generally went out on the suburbs of the city previous to the night intended for their departure and selected the place at which they were to assemble, never selecting the same place a second time, nor were more than two allowed to come in company to the place selected, and that in different directions, according to the advice of Mr. Torrey.

I had, at one time two more persons, in addition to the good friend Torrey already mentioned acting with me. Had I been a

Physiognomist,[35] I might, have been more fortunate in my selection, but not being acquainted with that science I was left to the mercy of every scoundrel who chose to feign himself a friend, hence the last mentioned individuals proved themselves to be polished villains.

One of them, by name George Lee, was appointed to conduct the people to the first place of deposit, and there give them into the care of a friend, who was to take them off his hands and conduct them about forty miles further and then give them in charge of another. Lee turned out to be both swindler and traitor for he went about among the slaves collecting money in my name from them, appropriating it to his own use, telling them that I would send them off at such and such times, without my having any knowledge of the fact. At length some of them became impatient and came to me and informed me that they had paid him sums of money with an understanding that I was to send them off; some of these I had before his face and he could not deny the fact, hence his villainy having being exposed, and he knowing that he had lost my confidence went on from one degree of rascality to another till he committed an act, the perpetration of which wounded my feelings more severely than any thing that had ever happened to me, and, which shewed a degree of ungratefulness and unreasonableness on the part of a man whose wife and two children I had so recently been instrumental in rescuing from the grasp of that boasting slaveholder, Bill Gunnell, whose watch word was, that a neger could not beat his time. That actually surpassed any thing I ever met with.

There were two men out on a scout, hiding and dodging from their owners, a friend of theirs came to me and requested I would try and get them off, but I could not hold out to him much prospect of my being able to get them away, inasmuch, as through the treachery of some of our brethren the way was so completely hedged up that it was impossible to get any one away at that time; but I promised him to do what I could. He then placed in my hands, for their use, a small sum of money while he kept the men concealed under his care. George Lee was a half brother to this friend of theirs, and he, learning that

I had the money, and wishing to get it for his own use, went to his brother who was anxious to get them off, and pretended he would get them away safe if he would let him have the money I had got, when in fact he knew he could do no such thing. However the friend of the men came to me, got the money, and gave it to Lee, his half brother, who instead of getting the men off safe took the poor creatures to the man, whose wife and two children had gotten off, and who was coachman for a gentleman in that city, and got him to take and conceal them in his stable loft, and feed them at his own expense, while Lee made use of their money, making him believe, at the same time, that I had it.

Of all this I was in total ignorance except the giving up the money, notwithstanding it was whispered about by the man, that he had the men, and was feeding them at his own expense, and I had their money and would do nothing for them. Now George Lee, without doubt, wishing to get out of this piece of rascality without myself or any one else knowing the game he had played, determined to betray the men into the hands of their masters; this, doubtless, he did by informing the slave catchers where they were; for a part of the very conversation the man had with Lee, the day previous, as repeated to him by the slave catchers at the time they took the men out of his stable loft; and notwithstanding this, and the part I had taken in the escape of his wife and two children, together with many others, he charged me with betraying them. I mention this with no unkind feeling towards him, or to wound his feelings, nor to revive old feuds, but it is necessary, because I afterwards received information from a friend which led me to believe that he was labouring under an erroneous impression that I still had those men's money, and that I had betrayed them for the same reasons which really had induced George Lee to do it, I therefore requested the man to whom I had returned the money, and my friend from whom I had received that information, together with the man, and Lee, to meet at my house without letting them know what my object was. They all met, and I then requested the friend of those men, who was as before stated half brother to Lee, to say if I had or had not returned to him the money I had received from him for the benefit of his friends, he said you did. The man then asked him what he had done with it; he said, I gave it to George Lee. He then asked Lee what he had done with it, he, with considerable confusion, acknowledged he had appropriated it to his own use.

Here then was a complete solution of the villainous game he had been playing. The same man also at that meeting wanted to know of Lee what he had done with some fifty or sixty dollars which he had collected from slaves, and put in his possession, for the purpose of conveying them away. This, it seems, he had also appropriated to his own use. This also led me into the light of something I had not before known. Now the fact is, that there was not a coloured man to be found, about there, who thought enough about the condition of his race as to make it a matter of study how he might assist to ameliorate their condition, or one who had the courage to try to do anything for them, yet, after I, who had made it a matter of study for years, had by the assistance of the Lord and Mr. Torrey opened a way through which scores were successful in their attempt to escape from slavery, there were plenty of championships of my own colour, who for the sake of filthy lucre attempted to build upon the foundation I had laid.

It appeared, that, that man, and others, thought that I was acting in what I was doing as agent for the abolitionists, hence for the purpose of supplanting me, they commenced a correspondence with my friend G. in Baltimore,[36] who acted the same part there that I did in Washington; but he would not listen to their false representations because he knew it to be an underhanded piece of business on their part, and that men guilty of such treachery could not be trusted with such ticklish operations. Besides they might have known (if my colour there could have been trusted with such secrets) that I was the establisher of that underground railroad, and that I was as independent of the Abolitionists in my operations as oil is of water, with one or two exceptions. And with regard to pecuniary aid afforded me by them it was not the amount of one farthing.

But with this drama my troubles did not end, for they proceeded against me from one degree of rascality to another trying to entrap me, and at the same time to appear innocent of the deed. But I was aware of their stratagems and was by the assistance of the Lord enabled as it were to escape by the skin of my teeth.

But I will proceed to notice another remarkable piece of treachery, perpetrated by Benjamin Lannum. I had seen a reward offered in the papers for the apprehension of a slave who had absconded from his owner, taking with him a considerable amount of money, doubtless his own earnings. This man lingered about the neighbourhood of his owner, unable to effect his escape, till at length hearing of me he employed a man, by the name of Franklin, who came about twenty-five miles to obtain my assistance in effecting his escape.

With a great deal of reluctance, owing to the difficulties which lay in the way through treachery, I consented, after charging him not to bring any but the man and two others whom he said he wished me to take. He was particularly cautioned to bring no females, because the difficulties to be encountered made it impracticable to have any with me. Besides, it was only the precarious situation of the first-mentioned man, that had more weight with me than the dangers with which I had to contend in effecting his escape. However I appointed the time and place at which Franklin was to meet me, with the three men, which was at eight o'clock on the succeeding Saturday night, at the shore of the eastern branch of the Potomac,[37] opposite to Washington. I then engaged a confidential friend, whom I shall ever hold in grateful remembrance for his fidelity, to accompany me in a boat to the place above mentioned.

Franklin met us there, but not according to agreement with regard to time, nor to the persons he was to bring; for instead of eight o'clock, he did not arrive till twelve; and then he brought only two men and a woman; leaving behind the very man whose case induced me to undertake the enterprise. Eight o'clock had been chosen in order to give time to reach the city and have the people concealed before the ringing of the bell for ten o'clock,[38] at which time every coloured person, no matter how respectable, had to be in doors; or, if taken, be carried to the lock-up house, and next morning, if free, pay a fine of five dollars or go to the workhouse; if a slave, the master to pay a fine of five dollars or the slave receive as many lashes on the bare back. However, being thus belated, I so managed as to reach the city by four o'clock in the morning, it being between day break and day light, at which time the watch retired from the duties of the night.

I had given notice to Benjamin Lannum of what was going on because he was the person who had attended to the fugitives that I had concealed from time to time; I, therefore, on reaching the city, proceeded with the people in the direction of the place where I intended to conceal them, calling at the dwelling of Lannum on my way, and after giving proper directions relative to the men and woman, I gave them into his charge, and retired to my home after being out all the night. On reaching home I found Franklin there; I pressed upon him the absolute necessity laid on him to bring the man he had left behind within my reach, because his case was almost desperate; besides, he had received twenty-five dollars of that man's money, for services which would not be performed until he brought the man to me. I had discovered also that the men whom Franklin brought, had, by some means or other, possessed themselves of all the man's money, and were desirous of making their escape to the north, leaving him to his fate, whatever that might be, so that they might have the money for themselves.

I cannot but believe that Franklin was privy to that infamous design, which I was determined not to be a party to, if possible, to carry out. I told Franklin that I would wait until the following Wednesday, so as to give him ample time to find the man if he was disposed so to do. In the meantime I intended to go as far as Baltimore and acquaint my friend G. of what was doing, and to obtain his assistance when I should arrive in that city with the fugitives; and then return to Washington and start with the people for the north, on the Wednesday night before mentioned.

But all my designs were frustrated, through treachery, and

myself like to have been entrapped. Franklin, however, after taking breakfast at my table, started for home, and after crossing the river and proceeding about two miles met the man, and notwithstanding he had received twenty-five dollars for his services, he would not return to me with him until the poor fellow had agreed to give him twenty dollars more, which I paid to him, on his return to me with the man, out of a hundred and fifty dollars that had been placed in my hands, by one of the first two men he had brought, for the expense of the jaunt.

He brought the man to my house the same day, which was sabbath, about eleven o'clock, and it being church-going time of the day they were not noticed more than other persons. I kept him at my house until near six o'clock, because at that hour crowds would be again going to the churches, and he could pass to the place where the others were concealed, without being much observed. For that purpose I sent my good friend who had assisted me across the river with the others, to Lannum, about six o'clock, to inform him that the man left behind had come, and that I wished him concealed with the others, but to my great surprise and consternation he returned to me with the information that the fugitives had been taken by Williams, the slave trader, soon after they had been concealed, which was early in the morning.

Notwithstanding this, Lannum never gave me information of the fact until I sent my friend to him, about six o'clock, for the object above mentioned, which, with other circumstances, proved that Lannum gave Williams information of their whereabouts; besides, it was said that a woman saw him go towards Williams' dwelling, saw also a window hoisted, and a conversation held between him and Williams. Of this the woman upbraided him at a chapel the same day; not only so, without suspicion on my part yet with some surprise, it was not over an hour after I had parted from him and the fugitives before he was at my house for the money I had agreed to give him for taking care of them until I got them away.

The amount I gave him was thirty dollars. This sum may seem large to those unacquainted with such operations, but for that want of sympathy with each other that exists among us, I, on various occasions, had to pay some of them considerable sums to get them to act on behalf of our suffering brethren, and this was a case in point, though it did not prevent treachery.

Fortunately for myself, the persons thus betrayed by Lannum, could not describe me to the slave catchers, for I was only with them in the dark, although they could call my name; yet as there were other Smallwoods in Washington, they could not find the guilty one, therefore I escaped the snare laid for me in that piece of treason. Lannum, of course, through policy, did not point me out, for he tried very hard to have me believe he was not guilty of the crime, and indeed I dared not charge it home to him, for I was, as I had been for some time, between two fires—my own colour, on the one hand, through envy and for the sake of filthy lucre were trying to betray me; while on the other hand, the slaveholders were offering large rewards for the detection of the person or persons who were thus robbing them of their goods and chattels.

There was another circumstance which aggravated my precarious position, among some of my colour. I had a controversy with a coloured man, a preacher, by name Abraham Cole,[39] growing out of a rebuke I gave him in a leaders' meeting, in consequence of his improper walk,[40] consequently his friends strove to do me all the injury they could by making use of the most disreputable means to accomplish their object. They would try to make it appear among the respectable portion of my own colour, that I was a great traitor to my race, by circulating the most absurd falsehoods about me; while on the other hand, they would try underhandedly to point me out to the slaveholders as being the man who was aiding in the escape of their slaves; but by the assistance of the Lord I so far evaded all the snares set for me.

But the scene of difficulties did not end with these: seeing that through the treachery of some of my colour I could be of no further service to my poor slave brethren, and that the cloud of treachery began to thicken, and get blacker and blacker over me, and that Washington was no longer a place of safety for me, I determined to seek a resting place in some other clime, and I was convinced that the place could only be found in America, to my satisfaction, in the British dominions, where the laws are equal, and know no difference between man and man on account of colour; therefore, to accomplish that object, I set out from Washington, 30th, of June, 1843.

I passed rapidly on my journey without stopping to hold any parley with Abolitionists or any one else, except in Philadelphia and Albany, to explain away some falsehoods left at those places by miscreant fugitives, and which, as usual, were too eagerly swallowed by some Abolitionists. On the fourth day of July I arrived at Toronto, in Canada; and how different were my feelings that day[41] to what they would have been had I been in the States. There I would have been compelled painfully to witness as I had done for many years their hypocritical demonstrations in honour of a day, which they say, brought to them freedom; but I sorrowfully knew that it was in honour of a day that brought to me, and my race among them, the most degrading, tyrannical and soul-withering bondage that ever disgraced the world or a nation.

But here, I was on Canada's free soil, and I may rejoice and give thanks to God in honour of that day, it being the day on which I first put my feet in a land of true freedom, and equal laws. Having visited several places in Canada, I speedily returned to Washington, there to have another contest with slaveholders, and treacherous coloured persons, and prepare to take leave of that mock metropolis of freedom, and sink of iniquity. On arriving there, I learned that it was rumoured about that I was the person that was getting away the slaves and that my visit to the North was to make arrangements to further that object; I found it therefore necessary to make speedy arrangements for leaving.

But in consequence of false information having been given by James Williams, a slave, to Charles Miller, a butcher, to the effect that I was about to leave for Canada and with me take a number of slaves, among whom, a woman belonging to the said C. Miller, my house was surrounded early on the night preceding the morning I was to start with my family, by the watch, and Goddard, their Captain at their head.[42] I was seated in the front door when a police man with whom I was acquainted came to me and said, "Thomas I have been instructed in consequence of information that you intend starting for Canada with some slaves to come and search your house," I invited him to do so, after doing so he left the inside of the house but did not leave the premises until searching the house a second and third time, the last of which the blackguard Goddard came in and said, "Smallwood, I understand you are going off to Canada and intend to take slaves with you."

He then proceeded to examine those in the house as to whether they were chattels or free negroes; there were ten or twelve persons present in the house at the time preparing to leave for Canada the next morning, and take a final leave of such beautiful scenes of republican freedom. It is true that I had another slave woman concealed in my house and for whom I for sometime had been trying to make a way of escape, but I had no intention of taking this woman or any other slaves with me, for I had made arrangements with confidential friends to take and keep her until a way of escape could be made. But to get her out of the house unperceived was a matter of great importance. However, that was speedily accomplished by some females, who took her through a back door into the garden, and concealed her in some corn.

On the 3rd day of October, 1843, with considerable difficulty, I got my family on board the steamboat Columbia, for Baltimore; intending myself to remain in Washington that day, to dispose of some furniture, at auction, and then take the cars the next morning, for that city, which would have conveyed me there at the same hour the steamboat arrived. But I was assailed on my way down to the boat, with my family, by two constables and an Irishman of the name of Kennedy. A relative of George Lee lived with Kennedy, to whom Lee had revealed all my operations, and he revealed the same to Kennedy, therefore he could tell me as much about my operations as if he had witnessed them personally. His object was, however, to obtain from me twenty-nine dollars and some cents, the amount of a note which I had endorsed to take a man out of gaol, but which was not due for some time, but I paid it.

Kennedy intimated at the same time that I ought to pay a certain amount to prevent my being arrested on the charges preferred against me. The constables however declined to arrest me then, saying they had no warrant to do it, but I was aware that if I returned to the house to get the furniture I had left to dispose of at auction as I had intended, I would be arrested through the information given by Kennedy, I therefore instead of returning sought a place of concealment for that day.

About four o'clock the next morning I set out on foot, on a by-road, for Baltimore, not daring to attempt a passage on the cars, I doubted not that the constables were looking out for me; they doubtless having had knowledge of my original design to take the cars that morning. I would have set out earlier, but my place of concealment was within the limits of the city, and I did not think it safe to start until four in the morning that being the time the watch retired from duty.

I reached Baltimore at five o'clock the same day and found my wife and children; she had undergone much uneasiness on my account, notwithstanding she had sufficient presence of mind to make arrangements to remove the only obstacle that lay in the way of our obtaining a speedy passage out of Baltimore, the last place of danger to me. The time had been that it was only necessary for a coloured person to present a paper purporting to come from the office of the county clerk, having the seal of the said county stamped on it, and a description of the person, certifying the bearer to be a free negro, to obtain a conveyance on any of the public highways. But at that time it was not so, in consequence of several instances of stage and steamboat proprietors being sued and mulct in for the value of slaves that were proved to have absconded on their conveyances. Hence to anticipate any contingencies in that way, the proprietors of public conveyances in the slave states required coloured persons presenting themselves for a passage to procure a responsible person or persons to enter bond to the amount of the value of the person or persons wishing to procure a passage. By the time therefore that I had reached Baltimore my wife had gotten over that difficulty through the kindness of Mr. Pitman,[43] an excellent gentleman of English parents, who signed a bond to the amount of two thousand dollars as the value of myself and family.

I had forwarded a letter to some friends in Albany, N. Y., informing them of my condition, and letting them know that I was separated from my wife and children, and the probability was that I should not be able to join them before reaching Philadelphia or New York, and that they were short of money. Leaving Baltimore, Thursday evening, seven o'clock, we reached Albany about twelve o'clock, Saturday, and found that those friends to whom I wrote had employed a man to meet my family, and to take charge of them; a kindness on their part I shall ever hold in grateful remembrance, especially Messrs. Croker, Thomson and Latimore, of Albany, N. Y.[44] I mention these, because of their unbounded benevolence to fugitives, falling in their way.

There are other bright stars of benevolence in that City, the names of whom are too numerous to mention. Notwithstanding their kind offers to assist me in business, I declined to settle there. I pushed on for Canada, and arrived at Toronto, October 14, 1843, and settled in it, and I have never regretted one moment for having carried out my first intention, which was, inasmuch as I had to leave the metropolis of the United States, to seek freedom, from whose legislative halls freedom is proclaimed to all the world, except to the African race, I would seek it in no part of that inconsistent nation, because I was aware that there was no freedom for a coloured person within its limits.

I was only a few days in Toronto, before I was solicited by four men, Osburn Turner, James Woodland, Stephen Brown and Levi Scott, (the last three were a part of some of the gangs gotten away by me from Washington) to try and get their wives and children, who were in Washington, to them. I consented to do so, and for that object I got up a subscription list, and started for the States, and after trudging about Western New York, three weeks, I reached Albany, only having obtained about forty dollars, for I found the Abolitionists more willing to give their thousands to a defunct institution, got up by a few designing persons[45] in the name of coloured refugees in Canada, but in reality, I believe, to line their own pockets, than to give a few shillings to get those families to their husbands. (I mean the Dawn.) The coloured people, as a body, in Canada, will never appreciate the benevolence, if benevolence it may be called, of those who gave large sums of money and quantities of clothing in their name, and that against their will, to enrich those who constituted themselves the managers therein.

I had written to Mr. Torrey about four weeks previous to my arrival in Albany, informing him that I was trying to collect money, and for what object, requesting him at the same time to forward a letter to a certain friend in Washington, desiring him to send the above mentioned families to Philadelphia; this he did, but he had also conceived the following scheme, that we should try and obtain a team and proceed to Washington, and bring away as many slaves as we could. For the accomplishment of that I was furnished with a second subscription list (having given the first together with the money collected into the hands of Mr. Torrey) with which I spent another week trying to collect more money for the furtherance of the enterprise we had in view, but with poor success.

In the meantime however, thirty dollars were sent to Mr. Torrey from Vermont, to be applied in trying to get the wife and child of James Baker, a young man whose escape we had effected, and whose good conduct had won for him the good wishes of some of the good people of that State. With this, and that which I had collected, we departed on a certain Friday evening, from Albany, for New York City, and arrived there on Saturday morning. From thence we proceeded to Philadelphia, arriving there on the evening of the same day, and stayed there over Sunday.

One circumstance I ought to have mentioned in connection with Lannum's treachery, previously mentioned, but which I notice here. William Nichols, a preacher of the African M. E. Church, was sick on his death bed, (though he did not, I presume, suppose himself so near death's door,) and I called to see him, and while there I communicated to him some of the circumstances connected with the capture of those people, which he twisted into a wicked falsehood, and as I have been informed, died with it on his lips, that I betrayed those persons, and that lie was the only testimony he left of his acceptance with God; a poor one indeed. Therefore, on arriving in Philadelphia, I met with the outrageous falsehood for the first time. Mr. Paine, a preacher of the same denomination[46] as Nichols, and at that time stationed at Washington, became the devil's packhorse, and bore the falsehood to that City.

On Monday we started for Wilmington, Delaware, and arrived there the same day, and put up at that excellent gentleman's, Mr. Thomas Garrett's.[47] The next day, Tuesday, we put out for Kennett Square,[48] in Pennsylvania; there we obtained a wagon and span of horses and proceeded the same day for Maryland, and in the night, of the same day, reached a tavern near Mason's and Dixon's line, and put up for the night. Early the next morning we were off again for Baltimore, and after driving all day and late at night, we arrived in Baltimore, at about eleven o'clock.

The next morning we expected the four families we had written for, I therefore set out in pursuit of them, in the direction of the dock, where the Steamboat from Washington lay, and met two of them, the other two having declined to come. After making the necessary arrangements for their departure to Philadelphia, we again started for Washington at two o'clock the same day, and arrived there at eleven o'clock the same night, and stopped at friend John Bush's, who had, according to our request, made the necessary arrangements for carrying out the enterprise.

We kept ourselves very close the next day, intending to start at night with our chattels, about fourteen in number, but unfortunately for us the police of that city had been made aware of our coming, therefore while I was harnessing the horses in the stable, and Mr. Torrey was doctoring the people in the wagon, a friend came to me, and said, "friend Smallwood, I see some white men standing out there on the hill side and they look like constables." I immediately communicated the same to Mr. Torrey, who said to me, I will go and see; he soon returned to me trembling, and saying they were constables and requested me to try and get the people out of the wagon, they were ten in number; but he soon said to me, you can't, they are closing on us; therefore we had to make speed in making our own escape and leave the poor creatures to the mercy of the bloodhounds. After getting about a quarter of a mile from the place I heard the clanking of the chains, and shrieks of the poor souls, but we could afford them no help, they were in the claws of the lions.

Mr. Torrey and myself became separated from each other during our flight. In the meantime, I fell in with a particular friend, who said to me go home with me and stay and rest yourself until to-morrow night, and then start, but I thanked him and declined his kind offer, and told him I would not stop until I reached Baltimore, for that while they would be ransacking Washington, thinking I was still there, I would be far away out of their reach.

So I took leave of him just as the bell began to ring for ten o'clock, at which time all coloured persons had to be in doors, and pushed forward for Baltimore, steering clear of every dwelling on the road by taking a circuitous route, fearing that the dogs might be roused, and that they might rouse the inmates, and I myself be attacked for a fugitive. For I knew that if I was I should be lodged in gaol for a fugitive, and my case would be hazardous, for I had left my free papers at home, in Toronto; not thinking when I left that I should go into any of the Slave States; and they were not then required in any of the so-called Free States.

However, I reached Baltimore the next morning, Saturday, about eight o'clock, and kept a close house at my friend G's until that day week. Mr. Torrey did not come for three or four days after the catastrophe, but remained in Washington to make arrangements with Mr. Hall, a lawyer,[49] for the defence of our friend John Bush, from whose premises we were routed, and the people taken; for which he was arrested.

Monday morning, being the first issue of the Baltimore Sun[50] after its editor had information of the affair, it contained a detailed account of the matter, from a correspondent in Washington, to the following effect, "Information having been received by the police of this city, that a negro fellow by the name of Thomas Smallwood, who had removed to Toronto, Canada, a few months ago, and a white man, arrived in this city on Thursday night, about eleven o'clock, with a team, for the purpose of taking away a number of slaves; a strict look out was kept, and on Friday night the wagon with the horses and a number of slaves were taken, but Smallwood is not yet captured."

This shewed me, as I had anticipated, that they were on the wrong scent, and that while they were beating the air and moving heaven and earth as it were to find and arrest me, in Washington, I, by the assistance of the Lord, was far away out of their reach. Mr. Torrey was not molested during his stay in Washington; being a white man they dared not publish him, or bring any charge against him, because they were not sure that they could sustain it; and it would only have subjected them to legal action. But with regard to myself it was different, I was a coloured man, and so it made no difference; besides they had other charges against me which they could sustain. Mr. Torrey arrived in Baltimore from Washington the succeeding week, and afforded me the means to reach Philadelphia, for I had none, having delivered all I collected into his hands except what little I expended while collecting.

On the Saturday evening following the one on which I arrived in Baltimore I set out for Port Deposit, about forty miles from Baltimore, in company with my friend G. and a slave man, who was to accompany me to Philadelphia. Friend G. had to accompany me, as he did fugitives from slavery, because I had been published as a fugitive from justice, and was liable to be taken and carried back to Washington, where I should be tried, and if convicted, sent to the Penitentiary for fourteen years. Not only so, that was his part in the transaction of the underground railroad, and with which I was unacquainted.

A little south of Port Deposit bridge, on the road side, lived a woman whose name was Turner; this woman had been in the habit of keeping fugitives for friend G. until friend P. from the other side, who kept a secret ferry, would come and take them, and conduct them, on his part of the road, into Pennsylvania, and deliver them to the protection of the Quakers; but she had turned traitress and had betrayed some into the hands of their owners, therefore it was necessary to keep clear of her. In order to do this we thought to pass her house before daylight, so as not to be seen, but when we got opposite the house, to our surprise, who should be standing at the window looking down on us but the old dame herself; she being so used to friend G's movements, it was hard to delude her.

We passed on, however, and crossed the bridge just at the rising of the sun, and went to friend P's, and there put up for the day. We remained there until six o'clock in the evening. At which time the house was beset by constables from that den of slave catchers, Havre de Grace, a village near Mason's and Dixon's line. They were doubtless made acquainted with our whereabouts by Mrs. Turner, who knew as well as we did, where we stopped. The slave who was with us, at their first approach, went out of the house into the road, whom they interrogated as to who he was, and where he was from, and then made a rush in the house, evidently in search of me, but as the house stood at the foot of a mountain, and had several rooms in it, I, while they were searching one, slipped through a secret door, which had been put there for such purposes, and was soon lost to them in the thick bush that covered the hill.

There was considerable snow on the ground it being in December, but I went on all night trudging through the snow, up hill and down hill, over streams and through plains in a part of the country I knew nothing of. My object, of course, was to reach Pennsylvania, and at about, three o'clock in the morning I thought I might be in that State, therefore I ventured to hail the inmates of a small house on the road side and inquired what county I was in, and if there were any coloured people living in that vicinity, for I did not wish to be, thought a fugitive by inquiring whether I was in Pennsylvania or not.

However the answer satisfied me that I was in that State, it also informed me that opposite there lived two coloured families whose houses I could see through a little skirt of bush that intervened, so I bore away for them; passing by the first, I rapped at the door of the second, and after answering to the call, "who is that?" and telling my story, the door was opened and I received a hearty welcome. I was not long in the house before I let them know that I wanted something more than being let in, and warmed by two fires, one in a stove, and one in a chimney or fire place, between which I had snugged myself, for I had eaten nothing since the previous morning, and of that I very quickly let them know, upon which the daughter of Ezekiel Clark (for that was the name of the good man of the house) a handy good looking young woman cheerfully arose from her bed and ministered to my necessity.

I learned there that the nearest railroad depot for Philadelphia was fourteen miles, so after being prevailed on to take a little more to eat, I set out about nine o'clock for that place to take the cars for Philadelphia, and reached it a little before six in the afternoon: taking the cars at six o'clock I was in Philadelphia by nine o'clock the same evening. After spending one day there, during which I occupied my time in listening to the debates in an anti-slavery convention, then assembled in that city, the anti-slavery committee received a dispatch from Mr. Torrey,* urging that I should leave immediately for other parts of the North; that the slaveholders were in hot pursuit of me; therefore I took passage on board of a steamer for Albany, N. Y., on my way to Canada.

The reader may remember that we met two of the four fam-

*I left Mr. Torrey in Baltimore, Maryland, in December, 1843; he was, if my memory be not at fault, arrested in July, 1844, in Baltimore, on a demand of the Governor of Virginia upon the Governor of Maryland, to be delivered over to the authorities of the former under a charge of bringing out of Virginia two children to their mother, into a land of freedom. Pending his examination under that charge there was another preferred against him, of having accomplished the escape of a woman with her two children out of Baltimore, into a land of freedom; this latter charge having been established to the satisfaction of the slaveholders, it took the precedence of the first; so that the Virginia claim fell until the Maryland law was satisfied, by his incarceration for six years in the Maryland State Prison. Had not death terminated his earthly career before his term of imprisonment expired, in all probability he would have been handed over to the tender mercies of Virginia, to satisfy her slave laws.

ilies spoken of in a preceding part of this narrative, whom we sent to Philadelphia, to remain until we returned; they also accompanied me, but as none of us had any money with which to travel, though I was known they were not, the anti-slavery committee anticipating that they would have difficulty in raising means to get along, furnished the females with a paper, purporting that they were fugitives from bond slavery, whereas they were not, but which delusion I was not at liberty to dispel.

So we travelled on slowly, getting a little here and there, and to make up the deficiency I made use of what little I had, which was only six dollars, that had been given to me for my own use. Our means however, not being sufficient, I sold my watch in Buffalo to get them to Toronto, which city we reached on the 23rd of December, 1843, in the steamer Transit. I mention the steamer, because Capt. Richardson,[51] according to his usual benevolence reduced the fare for us.

Now with regard to the advantages that would accrue to the coloured people if they settled in Canada, politically and domestically, they have been kept in total ignorance, and our abolition friends on the other side have contributed not a little to that ignorance, for I would be greatly annoyed when with great danger to my own freedom I had got off slaves and advised them to go to Canada, to hear when they had got north, they had been induced by the abolitionists not to go to Canada; that they told them the most absurd stories about it imaginable, and promised them perfect freedom and safety in the Northern States;—whereas they knew they could do no such thing.

Added to that, many persons of my own colour came to Canada, and because they could not live in idleness and laziness, returned to the States, and made unfavourable reports about Canada. These tales were eagerly swallowed by others of my own colour in the States, as being true, instead of coming to see for themselves. Now, as a general rule, there can be no better evidence of the worthlessness of coloured people than when they leave Canada and go to the States, and give it a bad name, and say they cannot live in it. It is a remarkable fact, of which our white fellow subjects have not been idle observers, that hitherto the coloured population of Canada, in the general, have been an industrious and sober class of people; and this is owing to the circumstance that when any worthless and idle ones came to Canada they found no encouragement for their lazy and idle habits; hence they make back tracks for the States, and I pray God that none such may ever find a resting place in Canada.

But on the other hand, I would say to every sober, industrious coloured man, in the States, come to Canada, and you will get freedom, yea British freedom! which is the best national freedom in the world! But the policy which has been pursued by our abolition friends in persuading the fugitives to settle in the Northern States has been attended with the most disastrous consequences; they appealed to the hopes and fears of the poor fugitives, and made them believe that Canada was one of the most frightful spots on the globe; by this means thousands were induced to settle in the Northern States who have now by the passage of that iniquitous fugitive law[52] [been forced] to break up, sacrifice what little they had accumulated, and fly to Canada, and begin anew. Whereas, if they had been encouraged, or even let alone, they would have gone to Canada at first, and be now secure in their persons and property as British subjects.

Besides, another consequence growing out of that policy was, that the great accumulation of fugitives in the Northern States was a great annoyance to the slaveholders, who, coming North annually, would either see or hear of their own or neighbour's slaves, who had escaped from them, but whom they could not conveniently capture. But at length, knowing their power and influence over the North, they determined to have a law by which they could make their northern vassals the captors of their fugitives. Now, if that accumulation had been in Canada, I opine that there could have been no wish for that law on the part of slave-holders, and certainly not on the part of others, knowing that it could have no effect on any part of the glorious empire of Britain.

I do not wish however to attribute national motives to the

whole body of abolitionists in the States, for such a course, for I believe many of them had a fond, though vain hope, of seeing a day when the coloured race in the United States would be admitted to equal rights with the whites; but I believe that national prejudice may be attributed to a very large portion of them. It is a part of the principles ingrafted in their national compact, and have been carried out to the present time, without abatement, that the African race should never ascend to an equality with the whites.

Not content with inoculating the length and breadth of their own land, with that infernal principle, they have the audacity to attempt to insert it into foreign countries, and if Canada had not been an integral part of the glorious British empire, they would have succeeded in it to their utmost wishes. But the Lord be thanked for the existence and maintenance of such a just and powerful nation;—she has triumphed, to the great annoyance of her enemies, and will continue to do so, while she pursues the just and righteous course she has hitherto pursued;—"Righteousness exalteth a nation, but sin is a reproach to any people."

It was to the abolitionists that the fugitives, fresh from the hotbeds of slavery, were directed to obtain assistance and advice on their way to Canada; and notwithstanding they knew that every coloured person going to Canada, and conducting themselves right, would enjoy as perfect freedom as they themselves, yet they would strenuously persuade and insist on them to settle in the so-called Free States. They could not but have foreseen the evil that has come upon the fugitives in the States from the influence that slavery had over the entire union, of which they were not ignorant. I saw it, and warned my brethren in the States of its approach. Besides, the dexterity of the slaveholders, and their northern vassals, in bringing Texas into the Union a Slave State, and the frequent attempts on the part of the United States government to negotiate with Great Britain for the delivery of fugitive slaves, who should take refuge in British territory, was, I think, sufficient to convince the most superficial observer of events, that the slave power would finally triumph through the whole union.

Now then, in view of these remarks, I beg leave to adhere to my opinion, that a large portion of the abolitionists of the United States, who, with these evidences before them, must have been actuated by national prejudices in persuading the fugitives to stop in the States. I was informed by parties who came to this city last winter, that after the passage of the fugitive bill, the coloured people of a town in which they lived were making ready to leave in a body for Canada, but the white citizens called meetings and vehemently insisted on them not to leave, that they would protect them at all hazards, consequently many were foolishly induced to remain. But as soon as the winter set in, and travelling became difficult, it was whispered about the town among the whites that the negroes, in that place, were to be carried back to slavery; and they were coolly told by those who had induced them to stop, that they could do nothing for them.

The United States is the most hypocritical, guileful, and arrogant nation on the face of the earth. It is far preferable for coloured people to be subjects of any other nation on earth than that. Its people rend earth and air with their protestations of freedom! They taunt other nations with tyranny! They hold large mass meetings and make declamatory speeches against other nations; and openly collect funds to assist the subjects of other nations to rebel against their governments. They send out emissaries among the people of other nations to emit their poisonous principles. They compass sea and land to make proselytes; and when made, they are worse if possible than they are themselves: for I declare from my own knowledge, that foreigners, who become slaveholders in the States are more cruel than the natives.

Out of many, I will mention a case or two in point. I knew an Irishman, while I lived in Washington, who was superintendent of the government grounds, attached to the President's house,[53] and the capital, who had several slaves, among whom was a young man whom he struck on the head with a bar of iron, which soon caused his death. He was suspected of it, but there was no direct evidence at the time. There was a young miss, however, either coming from or going to school, who saw it through a board fence, but said nothing about it at the time; but she frequently related the circumstance after she grew to be a woman, and among others she told it to Mr. Torrey. One of his slaves I had the pleasure to deprive him of and she is now in this city.

Again, I knew a Scotchman, Turnbull was his name, he was so severe to his slaves that they used to run off into the bush: one of them fled to the bush, in winter, and after being there a few days became so pinched with cold and hunger, that he determined to return to his master; but, through fear, he gave himself up to one Eatten, a slave-catcher, and requested him to intercede for him; Eatten went with him, and found his master's son at home; the old man not being at home, the son was for being down on him at once, but Eatten prevented him: but when the master came, the first sight he had of the poor fellow, he up with a billet of wood and let him have it across the shoulder blade. Afterwards his mistress ordered him into her room, with some wood, and noticing his walk, she ordered him to take off his shoes and stockings to see what was the matter with his feet, in doing which his feet being so frosted the skin came off with the stockings; this, together with the shoulder blade being broke from the stroke his master gave him, terminated in his death.

The people of the United States arrogate to themselves the right to meddle with the affairs of others; but oh! if the Hon. George Thompson, or some other Philanthropist crosses the Atlantic to America, and raises his voice against the most inhuman system that ever blackened the pages of history, immediately there is a hue and cry among them, "hands off,"—"no foreign interference."

Now then I will give my opinion of the United States, caring not who may demur thereto, nor what may be said thereof. In the first place, I premise that the people of the United States will never voluntarily grant the African race among them freedom. Secondly, I liken them to the Egyptians on the one hand, and to the Jewish nation on the other. First then, God will not scourge or punish nations no more than he will individuals before he gives them due and faithful warning of the consequences of their repeated and manifold sins, and give them a space for repentance, that they may turn from the error of their ways; that they might cease to do evil, and learn to do well; while on the other hand, if they refuse to repent in the day of grace that is given them to follow after righteousness, Jer. viii. 20,[54] then does he leave them in their folly to work out their own destruction;—Isa. lxvi. 4, "I also will choose their delusions, and will bring their fears upon them; because when I called, none did answer; when I spake, they did not hear: but they did evil before mine eyes, and chose that in which I delighted not."

They fear their slaves will learn wisdom, and break off their fetters, and assert their freedom.—So they will. Neither will God be intreated in their behalf when they are thus left to themselves. See Jer. vii. 15; also chapters xi. 15, and xiv. 11. For then they have sinned unto death: see the first epistle of John, v. 16. Secondly, I shall draw an analogy between the United States and Egypt. Exodus iii. 7 & 8, "And the Lord said, I have surely seen the affliction of my people which are in Egypt, and have heard their cry by reason of their taskmasters; for I know their sorrows; and I am come down to deliver them out of the hand of the Egyptians;" and in the 10th verse, he says to Moses, "Come now therefore, and I will send thee unto Pharaoh, that thou mayest bring forth my people the children of Israel out of Egypt:" and in the 19th and 20th verses of the same chapter he tells Moses as follows, "And I am sure that the King of Egypt will not let you go, no, not by a mighty hand. And I will stretch out my hand, and smite Egypt with all my wonders which I will do in the midst thereof; and then he will let you go."

Hence their die was cast, and their destiny sealed: they had sinned out their day of grace, (as I believe the United States has;) therefore God had determined to punish them with an overthrow while delivering his people out of their grasp. Hence Moses and Aaron bore their mission to Pharaoh. That heathen King supposed that there was no higher power than that which his fathers, he, and his advisers had established in Egypt. "And Pharaoh said, Who is the Lord that I should obey his voice to let Israel go? I know not the Lord, neither will I let Israel go."

Exodus v. 2. So that instead of relaxation, they caused an increase of pressure on the people.

In like manner the rulers of the United States are acting. When the wise men, the sorcerers, the magicians, and astrologers of the United States were assembled at Washington, casting their rods in opposition to the servants of God, to see how they could further oppress the children of Ham, by opening a way through Mason's and Dixon's sea, that they might recapture those that had crossed, they attempted to expel from their hall a servant of God, the Hon. Mr. Seward,[55] for telling them that there was a higher power than their constitution. But many of the children of Ham, like the children of Reuben, Gad, and Manasseh, who took their inheritance beyond Jordan, Joshua xiii. 8, have taken inheritance beyond Lake Ontario: the result is, their oppressors are in hot pursuit to carry them back into bondage; but I believe that it will end in their overthrow, as it did the Egyptians at the Red Sea.

The Jews became proud, and puffed up, because God had chosen them for his peculiar people. Their great prosperity, as a nation, made them blind to their wickedness, and the sacred oracles, which God committed to them for the rule of their practice, they perverted to justify themselves in it. God, who, as before stated, will not punish his creatures before giving them due warning, and a further space for repentance, sent to them prophets, and teachers, of their own brethren; men of the greatest abilities; they had clear conceptions of the will of God concerning them, and they taught and warned their brethren against their unbounded wickedness, faithfully, that they should turn from their evil doing; but they revolted more and more; Isaiah i. 5: And killed the prophets and stoned them which were sent unto them and their land was left unto them desolate. Matthew xxiii. 37 and 38. So God blotted them out from among the nations of the earth.

Are not the United States in a similar position to that of the Egyptian and Jewish nations: they have been warned of their wickedness: their own brethren, of great abilities and virtues, have written and spoken to them against it, and warned them against the dreadful consequences that will inevitably overtake them if they continue to oppress the African race, and shed the blood of the Indians. But what has been their conduct, has it not been like that of the Jews? They have imprisoned all they could lay hands on, and otherwise persecuted them, even unto death. I believe the long suspended blow against that republic and the final emancipation of their victims are close at hand, and will be attended with a terrible and bloody breaking up of their present system.

No one knows nor can know the cruelties practised upon the slaves in the United States, but those who commit them, and the slaves themselves. The slaveholders are very careful to keep the world in ignorance of their brutalities to their slaves. Hence travellers going among them, being loaded with their hospitality, leave with an impression that slavery is not so bad as people say it is, whereas, they have not been permitted to look behind the scenes. Besides, the slaveholders make use of many arts to make strangers believe they are very good to their slaves, even to the mean practice (some of them) of taking a piece of meat skin, daily, and making their slaves grease the outside of their lips, and then take the same piece of skin and throw it up in the air to see which would be smartest in getting it to eat. This is done to have people believe they feed them well.

It can be nothing but the servile principle, for which the coloured people of the United States are so proverbial, that induces them to remain there, under its unequal laws. No matter how mean nor how bad the character (in the slave states) of a white person, his or her oath goes before that of a coloured person, no matter how respectable, nor how much he may have at stake. In a word, the oath of a coloured person is not allowed against a white person in any matter whatever; on the other hand, it only requires the oath of the meanest white person in that country, unsupported with any other evidence, to dispossess the most respectable coloured person of all he or she has.

It is true, the coloured people have as good a right to live in the United States, and enjoy the fat of the land, as their oppressors, but *"might overcomes right," where tyrants rule*. Did not our fathers fight side by side with their fathers, against the sires of the best friends they now have, to win that independence they now so much boast of? Yes, they did! And the only reward they received is a refusal on their part to permit them to enjoy a share of the freedom they had so nobly helped them to gain, and to oppress their children down to the last turn of the screw.

Yes, they even refused to grant a pension to the few shattered remains of those coloured regiments that fought so bravely in their continental army, and who received great credit from their officers. I knew one, by name John Carey; this man lived until he was one hundred and fourteen years of age, and in the hundred and thirteenth year of his life the magnanimous congress of the United States gave him a pension, which amounted to enough at the end of his life to bury him. The Rev. Obadiah Brown, a distinguished Baptist Minister, stated while addressing a congregation at his funeral, that he was in the whole of the seven years war during the revolution; sometimes fighting in the ranks, and at other times waiting on the person of Gen. Washington.

The coloured people have helped to clear their lands; worked their cotton, rice, sugar, and tobacco plantations. They have helped to build their cities, but it is not convenient for the coloured people to stay among them, because they oppress them; and it is a disgrace for them to stay when they can get away. Thank the Lord there is a land on the continent of America that they can get to, and have the best national freedom in the world, let who will say otherwise; where they may, through industry, prosper and multiply, until they become a terror to their enemies on the other side; and bid defiance to that much desired project, by some, (annexation); for no coloured person who has once tasted British freedom in truth and knows how to appreciate it, will tamely submit to have it transferred to their enemies, to have it dealt with according to their rule, for the gratification of a yankee loving faction, when they know so well what that rule is. They will present so formidable a front against annexation, that it can only be swept away with their lives.

They abolished the external or African slave trade, in 1808, the effect of which gave an impetus to the infamous traffic of slave breeding and trading among themselves;[56] and perhaps it was one of the main objects they had in view, the protection of their slave breeders and traders. I find, in a Liberty Party work, the following account of the export of slaves from 1830 to 1840, from seven of the old slave states, viz. Maryland, Virginia, North Carolina, South Carolina, Georgia, Kentucky, and Tennessee, to the new slave states, 431,278. According to Mr. Clay's average estimate, $400 for each slave, the whole amount of value for that number is put down at $172,511,200. Who can calculate the amount of suffering occasioned by the sudden snapping of conjugal and parental ties, among those poor creatures, by an unrighteous law, of that republic, for the gratification of about 248,711 slaveholders, in a nation of about 30,000,000?

Nothing but the day of judgment can bring it to light, when all secrets will be revealed with regard to the foregoing facts. It is hard to believe them sincere; although they have abolished the external slave trade, they have continued to nurture and foster an internal one. Besides, the supineness of the United States Naval Officers in suppressing the African slave trade,[57] is a manifest evidence that both they, and their government, connive at it. How many captures of slavers did they make between 1808 (that being the time they abolished the African slave trade) and 1840? not one I believe! Yet, between those periods I find it calculated in the above mentioned work, that the number of 3,880,000 were carried to Brazil, Cuba, Porto Rico, French Colonies, and the United States.

Now can any one believe that had not the American officers and their government connived at it they could have failed to make some captures in that time? I said to an American gentleman, in 1840, that while the British Officers were covering themselves with immortal fame in suppressing the African slave trade, the American Officers were covering themselves with immortal infamy, by doing nothing towards it. I asked him if he could tell me of a single capture of a slaver made by American Officers? But he did not nor could not tell me of one! No wonder, they connived at it; while some of their most distinguished men were only a few years ago engaged in the traffic; perhaps some are now.

I remember a few years since, in a debate in the United States' Senate, that a Southern Senator by way of retort upon Senator Knight, of Rhode Island,[58] stated the following circumstance in which his (Senator Knight's) colleague had been engaged; he was a great slaveholder, and slave trader, and on one occasion he had a cargo of slaves, and the small pox got among them, and in order to get rid of those, among his cargo, infected with it, he caused a plank to be laid across the gunwale of the vessel, near a balance, and then made the poor creatures walk out on it, and so they were cast into the sea. If any of the readers of this narrative remember a few years ago that a certain dignitary died in Providence, Rhode Island, whose coffin was ornamented with solid silver, and the vault was broken into and his coffin robbed of its ornaments, that was the man who committed that infamous act; a retribution for the way he got it; he robbed the poor Africans, and his tomb was robbed in turn, and it is well for him if he be suffering no other punishment for it.

One thing more, I should have noticed in another connection, the coloured seamen of the United States petitioned congress to protect them from imprisonment when they sailed to American and Spanish slave ports, but congress refused to receive their petition. Not long after the Americans expected to have gone to war with Britain, the coloured seamen being wide awake, knowing that they would want their services in their Navy, as they had before, held a meeting in New York City, and there passed resolutions recommending all coloured men not to enter the United States' service, in case of war. Some of them stated that 1500 coloured seamen lay in a British prison at one time, taken prisoners while fighting in the American service.

But the mist of American generosity has been dispelled from the eyes of the coloured people. The time was that the coloured people of the United States were easily deceived. In the last war with England, they had a good pretext to induce the coloured people to join their ranks, and not go over to the English, because they held slaves at that time also. They would tell their slaves that the English only wanted them to make sale of in the West Indies, for prize money; this deterred many, but some, having very cruel masters, ventured, believing no doubt that their condition could be made no worse, while there was a chance for it to be made better. And it was made better, as many of their descendants in Nova Scotia,[59] can testify.

No doubt there would be found some servile coloured men fighting in the ranks of the American army in case of war, as there was in the Mexican war: base fools! fighting for territory to perpetuate the slavery of their brethren. If I were in an army opposed to an American Army, I could have more sympathy for the men of any other nation, found in their ranks, than for those of my own colour, or race. And if such were the case, they might look for but little mercy from me, for I look upon such as a curse to our race, wherever found, and the sooner they are from among us the better.

The coloured men of the present generation are of no service to themselves, in the general, nor will they be to their posterity; and if their example be followed by their descendants, it will be a withering curse to them. They have neither energy nor courage. They are never found in unfrequented paths of enterprise. They are content to follow in the wake of the white man, and that very far behind; and to be hewers of wood and drawers of water, and hardly those.

If the example of a few of my coloured brethren, whom I visited at the Queen's Bush,[60] in 1843, was more generally followed by my coloured brethren in America, they would soon be worth something. Those men had settled there with no means whatever. They had to go fifteen miles out into the settlements, and there work for the farmers, a fortnight, to get provision sufficient to enable them to work one week in clearing their own land. And, while I was there, they were making their three meals a day on potatoes and salt; and this was their language to me, "friend Smallwood, you see how we have to live here, but we are willing to bear it, until we can get a foothold." I visited them again about three years after, the same men, some had four, some five, and some six hundred bushels of wheat in their barns, with a good portion of stock, and every thing else necessary for comfort around them. Thus, instead of having to go into the settlements to work for provision, they could hire men to work for them, and send their teams out with wheat, which brought them cash.

But how few of my brethren do I find possessed of a resolution like those men; instead of that, they are flying from city to city, seeking employment at the hotels, and steamboats; as waiters, cooks, and barbers. Their highest ambition is to be a good waiter, or barber, and then they are made. Even many of those who have obtained mechanical trades, have abandoned them, to follow those low callings; their trades being too high a degree for their low minds. Well might Walker say, in his Appeal, in reference to our race, in the United States, that, they "are the most degraded, wretched, and abject set of beings that ever lived since the world began, and I pray God, that none like us ever may live again until time shall be no more." I sanction his prayer, and say, amen, let it be so.

In closing this narrative, I very much regret that I have not the manuscripts of the various articles which appeared in the Albany Patriot, over the signature of Sam. Weller, in 1842 and '43, to append to this narrative, in addition to the letter appended; but being so beset by the slave hunters before I left Washington, I was compelled to destroy them, for fear of detection.

## APPENDIX.

There is one fact which I must notice, which I would not have done but under existing circumstances.—In 1847, Joseph Carter came to me while at a convention in Drummondville, C. W.,[61] with a due bill in his possession for a certain amount of money, which had been given to him in Scotland, for the purpose, as he informed me, of trying to get one or two sisters, with their children, out of slavery. He had left the money in the hands of a gentleman in Scotland, and as soon as he could get some one to consent to try and get them for him, he was to send the due bill for the money. He, therefore, requested me to undertake it for him; I refused, because I had had enough of getting slaves off, at the risk of my own freedom, with but little thanks, and a plenty of abuse. However, I referred him to Elder E. B. Dunlop, who was then acting as agent for the Anti-Slavery Societies of Canada West, but he did not undertake it.

About one year after J. C. applied to me again, and earnestly urged me to undertake the task for him; finally I consented, and advised him to get Mr. Peter Brown to send the due bill for the money, which he did, and he requested Mr. B. to hand over the money to me when it should come to hand, because he was living in the States. When the money came, I received $140, (leaving a balance of $60 in Mr. Brown's hands,) and paid it to Carter, and took his receipt for it, which I now have in my possession. We then went to Cincinnati, (that being at the line dividing Kentucky and Ohio, for they were in Kentucky when Carter left that State,) to consult some of the most active men of the underground railroad, as to the best mode of operation, in order to succeed in getting them; but every plan suggested on our part was considered impracticable, owing to the fact that a white friend of those whom we consulted had, not long before that, left Cincinnati with the intention to bring one hundred slaves out of Kentucky, and who was betrayed with that number near the line, or Ohio river, by two of the number, who gave him the slip, and informed against him, and he was taken with the slaves.

That circumstance deprived us of his assistance, while it also created so great an excitement and vigilance on the Kentucky side of the Ohio river, that after remaining eleven days trying to see what could be done, we were advised to return and wait for a more favorable time. I have letters from Cincinnati, now in my possession, in confirmation of the above statements.

## *Demoralizing Influence of Slavery.*

The demoralizing influence of slavery is seen among the whites and the blacks in the Slave States: for instance, behold the frequent resort that is had to pistols, swords, and bowie knives, among the Southerners; and the cold-bloodeds in affairs of (what they call) honor. They have not yet wiped away the stain of the blood of the venerable Professor Davis,[62] who was murdered a few years since by one of his students, for doing his duty towards him, for his good, by bringing him to just punishment. No! he was admitted to bail in the sum of $25,000, and sent out of the way until the bail was forfeited and paid by his wealthy parents; and so the matter ended, and a valuable life sold for $25,000, to gratify the blood-thirsty spirit of slavery.

With regard to the coloured people of the Slave States, the demoralizing influence of slavery is more particularly seen among the females, although it unavoidably extends to the males. For instance, female chastity among them is not protected by law, nor respected by the whites. Their virtue is tampered with, trampled on, violated; and is entirely at the mercy and will of any and every debauchee who chooses to arm himself with the advantages he has over the poor coloured female; and they are neither few nor far between.

Hence, there is no stimulation to virtue among the females; and the males, knowing that, are equally regardless of that great principle. For if one should chance to get a virtuous companion, her fidelity to him is almost sure to be destroyed by some white man. It matters not whether they be free or bond, the result is the same. The easy and luxurious life of the Southerners, by means of slave labour, disposes them to this species of vice. For the oppression of the African race in the south, the north need not think to escape the just punishment due to it; for the Northerners are the slave-holders, while the Southerners are the drivers, and they divide the spoil of their labour between them.

## *The Conduct of the Coloured People, in Canada, Impolitic.*

The policy of the Coloured People in separating themselves from the white religious connections in Canada, of whose persuasions they are, into distinct little bodies, is a bar to their moral and religious elevation, as well as to their domestic. I am free to admit that in the United States, where the laws make a distinction between the rights of the white and the coloured people, there were strong grounds for a separation, for the policy of the churches there is the same as that of the State: they deprive their coloured members of the rights enjoyed by their white members. That, unfortunately, has engendered a prejudice in the minds of many of the coloured people against being in connection with the white people.

But I warn my coloured brethren who are flying from their oppressors to these shores of freedom for all, and who are not only welcomed with out-stretched arms by our white brethren, who extend the hand of relief to their necessities, not to bring that spirit to this country; we want none of it here. The British people are not slaveholders! The British laws make no distinction between man and man on account of colour! It would be absurd, in the highest degree, for my strange brethren, who have sought freedom in this country, to seek to introduce and keep up a diabolical system that was forced upon them in a slaveholding country.

It is our business to identify our interest with that of our white fellow citizens, and to form the most intimate relations with them of which our circumstances in life will admit. They have, under God, all the wealth, influence, and power. How dare we then, poor refugees, to say, as I understand some have said, that, "they want nothing to do with the white people:"—the very people to whom they fly for freedom. We have neither learning, wealth, nor influence, at the present. It is to them, under God, that we owe our present freedom. With what grace, then, can we complain of prejudice against us, while we ourselves are the promoters thereof. There are too many among us who desire the chief seats in the synagogues, whose acquirements and talents are not sufficient to entitle us to them. They obtrude their ignorance upon the ignorance of their brethren, and thus the blind lead the blind.

* * *

The following letter is one of a number of letters written by me, between eight and nine years ago, from Washington, and published in the Albany Weekly Patriot, about that time, portraying the doings of the slave-holders. The assumed name, Samivel

Weller, Jr., was made use of to avoid detection; because a number of copies, of every issue of that paper containing those letters, were sent to each person of whom they treated. Those letters were a great annoyance to the slaveholders in that section, and they would have been very glad to have got the writer.

T. S.

## WASHINGTON CORRESPONDENCE.

### FREEMEN MADE SLAVES!—KIDNAPPING IN WASHINGTON!—MORE OF THE AUXILIARY GUARD!

For the *Albany Weekly Patriot.*

Washington, D.C.

June 6, 1843

*Mr. Editor,*—I have some things of much interest to communicate, that I write again sooner than I anticipated.

Twelve years ago a Mrs. Hardy, of Maryland, died, leaving all her slaves, by her will, to her brother, Basil Hatten, with a provision that they, with their increase, should be free at his death. There was a farther provision that, if any were not of age, they should be put to trades—the males till they were twenty-one, the females till they were eighteen.

Hatten died just about twelve years after his sister. The people being now free, many of them removed to this city.

Mr. Robert Hunter, the heir-at-law, claims as his slaves, all the children who were born between Mrs. Hardy's death, and the death of her brother, notwithstanding the clause in the will to free the "increase." He claims that they do not come under the provisions of the will, and that the "increase" refers to the children already born, at the time Mrs. Hardy died.

Some of them were pretty well advanced, though not of age. But he made no provision for them, nor attempted in any way to control them, with but one exception. He fooled one to remain with him on his plantation. The rest he could not deceive; so he cared nothing for them.

In order to carry out his designs against the children, he employed certain noted slave hunters in Maryland, to come to this city and kidnap them, which they did; six in number. They came on the SABBATH DAY, just about church time, that there might not be an uproar. They stole them, and carried them into Maryland. The case is now in law. The result is very uncertain.

This is not the only instance of kidnapping in Washington. I know a coloured man named Henry Chub, who sometimes worked about the dock, loading and unloading vessels. He, with two of his sons, had been unloading a vessel, and after discharging her, he went ashore, leaving his sons to clear out the hold of the vessel. In the meantime the captain set sail, and carried the two sons into slavery, to the unspeakable grief of their parents, who were both free born!

Similar acts have often been done, and are still doing, in this metropolis of free and christian America; whose free institutions (!!) are so much admired; and who keep God's children in abject slavery, and utter ignorance, with as much boldness as if an express command from God sanctioned the atrocity! Do Americans think that the rest of the world have not sense enough to see and despise their hypocrisy?

I come now to notice the death of a Christian and Patriot, in the person of JOHN CAREY. He died on the 2d ultimo, about nine o'clock, P.M. No person, I presume, in this city, has enjoyed a greater degree of the confidence of the public on account of his truly CHRISTIAN EXAMPLE. He was a member of the First Baptist Church. The body was brought into the meeting house, on the Sabbath afternoon, attended by several clergymen. The Pastor, Rev. Obadiah Brown, delivered an excellent discourse. He stated that Carey was born in Westmoreland county, Va., in 1729, as he had learned from documents that he had recently seen. This made him 114 years old next

August. Gen. Washington, who knew how to appreciate worth, in a black, as well as in a white man, chose him for his body servant. He was with him in the old French war, at Braddock's defeat and throughout the revolution. He was often in the ranks, helping to fight the battles of his country. At the close of the war, Gen. Washington gave him one of his regimental coats, which he always wore, especially on public occasions.

And what reward did the grateful Republic give him for his services? Why, a few months before his death, by the exertions of Hon. GEORGE N. BRIGGS, of Pittsfield, Mass., Congress was induced to pass a bill giving him a pension for the rest of his life. He received about enough to bury him decently! Most grateful country! Most magnanimous Congress!

I wish to bestow a passing notice on the AUXILIARY GUARD. Don't let the people forget these scoundrels! They have established a new branch of business;—it is, to station themselves in the streets, near the meeting houses of the coloured people, and watch if any are later than ten o'clock in returning home, to compel them to pay fines if they are free, or else send them to the work-house. If they are slaves their masters must pay, or they are whipped, for the CRIME of attending on the public worship of GOD, a few moments later than ten o'clock! JOHN LITTLE and WILLIAM COX are very active in this business. Little is too lazy to support his family in any other way; and he is as famous for administering discipline to his wife! as he is for negro hunting! How long will the people of the North agree to support these scoundrels?

You remember my telling you, that in the recess of Congress, the coloured people suffer much more than when Congress is here. It has been peculiarly so, since the last session. God help the poor defenceless ones!

Yours, for liberty.

SAMIVEL WELLER, JR.

# Suggestions for Further Reading

For background on the radical abolitionists of the nation's capital, including those who preceded and followed Smallwood and Torrey, Stanley Harrold's book *Subversives: Antislavery Community in Washington, D.C., 1828–1865* is highly recommended. For those who want to know more about Smallwood's younger partner, E. Fuller Torrey's biography of his distant relative, *The Martyrdom of Abolitionist Charles Torrey*, is well-researched and fair-minded. An excellent general history of the underground railroad, touching briefly on Smallwood and Torrey, is Fergus Bordewich's *Bound for Canaan: The Epic Story of the Underground Railroad, America's First Civil Rights Movement*, and a useful reference is Tom Calarco's *People of the Underground Railroad.*

There is little scholarship on Smallwood's writings, but a few articles are mentioned in the Introduction. *Flee North: A Forgotten Hero and the Fight for Freedom in Slavery's Borderland*, by the editor of this volume, is the only book-length treatment of Smallwood's life and writings. Here's to the hope that it will not be the last.

# Notes

## Introduction

1. **began to write himself into American literary history:** Most of the biographical facts and literary observations in this introduction are derived from the editor's 2023 book on Smallwood: *Flee North: A Forgotten Hero and the Fight for Freedom in Slavery's Borderland* (Celadon Books, 2023).
2. ***Pickwick Papers* had recently taken the reading world by storm:** For a discussion of the popularity of *The Pickwick Papers* and of its character Sam Weller, see Nina Martyris, "The Sam Weller Bump," *The Paris Review*, April 14, 2015, available online.
3. **extraordinary series of dispatches for a little abolitionist newspaper in Albany:** A nearly complete run of *Tocsin of Liberty* and the *Albany Weekly Patriot* have recently been digitized by the Boston Public Library and are available at Digital Commonwealth, www.digitalcommonwealth.org.
4. **He chose to call himself Samivel Weller:** Smallwood often renders the pseudonym as "Samivel Weller, Jr.," but there are numerous clues in the text that he is referring to Dickens's beloved character, and not a son of the character. In *The Pickwick Papers*, Samivel's father is named Tony Weller, but Dickens occasionally refers to Samivel as "Mr. Weller, junior." Smallwood also makes multiple references to Dickens (often by the nickname "Boz") as the author of a "memoir" of Samivel Weller and his father, Tony Weller; this "memoir" is *The Pickwick Papers*. For example, in *Tocsin of Liberty*, August 24, 1842, Smallwood writes: "The leading traits of the characters of my father and myself, as delineated by our biographer, Mr. Boz Dickens!"
5. **whose "walking property walked off":** *Tocsin of Liberty*, August 24, 1842.

6. **"The ignorant blunderhead!":** *Tocsin of Liberty*, September 7, 1842.
7. **In his newspaper pieces, Smallwood reported:** Smallwood's first use of "underground railroad"—and according to a search of newspaper databases, the first use in print—was in *Tocsin of Liberty*, August 10, 1842. Smallwood clarified that John Zell was the "constable" who had been overheard using the phrase in *Tocsin of Liberty*, November 3, 1842.
8. **"National Underground Railroad, Steam Packet, Canal and Foot-it Company":** *Albany Weekly Patriot*, June 15, 1843.
9. **"thus have perpetual slavery without danger":** *A Narrative of Thomas Smallwood*, p. 100 below.
10. **"I mean to tax them twice that, next year!":** *Tocsin of Liberty*, December 8, 1842.
11. **stated that the Weller letters were "written by me":** *Narrative*, p. 142 below.
12. **"The stupidity of some slaveholders is very great":** *Tocsin of Liberty*, August 24, 1842.
13. **"to get round a lazy, mole-eyed slaveholder":** *Tocsin of Liberty*, November 3, 1842.
14. **"Why, then, since the slave is happy":** Alfred L. Brophy, "Considering William and Mary's History with Slavery: The Case of President Thomas Roderick Dew," *William & Mary Bill of Rights Journal* 16, no. 4 (April 2008), p. 1123.
15. **"(alas! he could not read!)":** *Albany Weekly Patriot*, June 15, 1843.
16. **"Sophy you know, left Washington a year ago":** *Tocsin of Liberty*, November 3, 1842.
17. **Hanson "happens to think himself a man!":** *Tocsin of Liberty*, November 3, 1842.
18. **"Pray what should he 'call himself,' Mr. Gardiner?":** *Tocsin of Liberty*, August 24, 1842.
19. **"You see that the constitution and laws of our country afford":** *Albany Weekly Patriot*, August 22, 1843.
20. **"I would have been compelled painfully to witness":** *Narrative*, p. 117 below.
21. **David Walker, whose 1829 essay denouncing slavery:** The full title was *Walker's Appeal, in Four Articles; Together with a Preamble, to the Coloured Citizens of the World, but in Particular, and Very Expressly, to Those of the United States of America.* Available online at https://docsouth.unc.edu/nc /walker/walker .html.

22. **Morning arrived, and with it a terrible uproar:** *Narrative*, p. 106 below.
23. **It is true, the coloured people have as good a right:** *Narrative*, pp. 134–35 below.
24. **"I believe the long suspended blow against that republic":** *Narrative*, p. 134 below.
25. **chosen to write an "Address to the Colored Citizens of Canada":** *The Black Abolitionist Papers*, ed. C. Peter Ripley, vol. 2, *Canada 1830–1865* (University of North Carolina Press, 1986), p. 513.
26. **The *Narrative* was rediscovered in the 1980s by Henry Louis Gates, Jr.:** Gates, *Figures in Black: Words, Signs, and the "Racial" Self* (Oxford University Press, 1987), p. 131.
27. **The Mercury Press published a new, paperback edition:** Richard Almonte, ed., *A Narrative of Thomas Smallwood (Coloured Man)* (The Mercury Press, 2000). Almonte got a few details wrong—Joseph Smallwood was not Thomas Smallwood's son—but did some clever sleuthing in Toronto city directories. The book appears to be out of print and the website for The Mercury Press, which was subsidized by the Canadian government to publish Canadian authors, is no longer functioning.
28. **Hilary Russell drew extensively on the *Narrative*:** Hilary Russell, "Final Research Report: The Operation of the Underground Railroad in Washington, D.C., c. 1800–1860," The Historical Society of Washington, D.C., and the National Park Service, July 2001. See also Russell, "Underground Railroad Activists in Washington, D.C.," *Washington History* 13, no. 2 (Fall/Winter, 2001/2002), pp. 28–49.
29. **Sandrine Ferré-Rode wrote in 2013:** Sandrine Ferré-Rode, "A Black Voice from the 'Other North': Thomas Smallwood's Canadian Narrative (1851)," *Revue Française d'Études Américaines*, no. 137 (2013), pp. 23–37.
30. **Nele Sawallisch in 2018 published on Smallwood's radicalism:** Nele Sawallisch, *Fugitive Borders: Black Canadian Cross-Border Literature at Mid-Nineteenth Century* (Transcript Verlag, 2018), chapter 3.
31. **Bryan Sinche, in his study of self-publication:** Brian Sinche, *Published by the Author: Self-Publication in Nineteenth-Century African American Literature* (University of North Carolina Press, 2024), pp. 73–80.
32. **a paperback facsimile edition of the *Narrative*:** *A Narrative of Thomas Smallwood* (Cornell University Library Digital Editions, 2023).

33. **his pathbreaking 2000 article "On the Borders of Slavery and Race":** Stanley Harrold, "On the Borders of Slavery and Race: Charles T. Torrey and the Underground Railroad," *Journal of the Early Republic* 20, no. 2 (Summer 2000), pp. 273–92.
34. **E. Fuller Torrey, in his excellent 2013 biography:** E. Fuller Torrey, *The Martyrdom of Abolitionist Charles Torrey* (Louisiana State University Press, 2013), especially chapters 5 and 6.
35. **Tom Calarco in his many works on the underground railroad:** See in particular, Calarco's *People of the Underground Railroad: A Biographical Dictionary* (Greenwood Press, 2008), entry on Charles Torrey; Calarco et al., *Places of the Underground Railroad: A Geographical Guide* (Greenwood, 2011), pp. 352–53; and Calarco, *The Search for the Underground Railroad in Upstate New York* (History Press, 2014), chapter 4.

## THE "SAM WELLER" LETTERS

### *Tocsin of Liberty*, June 28, 1842

1. **Dear Goodwin:—Please reprint from the National Intelligencer:** Edwin W. Goodwin was in mid-1842 the editor of *Tocsin of Liberty*, the Albany newspaper where Charles Torrey would in a few months take the helm. The *National Daily Intelligencer* was a leading newspaper in Washington, D.C.
2. **"to beware of widows":** Smallwood is echoing a passage from Charles Dickens's 1837 novel *The Pickwick Papers* in which Tony Weller addresses his son, Samivel Weller, whose name Smallwood took as his newspaper pseudonym: "Take example by your father, my boy, and be wery careful o' widders all your life, specially if they've kept a public house, Sammy." *The Posthumous Papers of the Pickwick Club* (The Amalgamated Press Ltd., 1905), p. 258. For more on the background, style, and purpose of Smallwood's newspaper pieces, see Scott Shane, *Flee North*, chapter 7, and Stanley Harrold, *Subversives: Antislavery Community in Washington, D.C., 1828–1865* (Louisiana State University Press, 2003), chapter 3.
3. **the language of Boz:** Boz was a nickname for Charles Dickens, whose antislavery views appealed to Smallwood and whose influence on Smallwood's newspaper dispatches was profound.

## *Tocsin of Liberty*, July 27, 1842

1. **"General Forwarding Co.":** In a running joke in the pages of *Tocsin of Liberty*, Smallwood, along with the New York abolitionist Abel Brown and others, referred to their assistance to people escaping slavery as the work of a freight-forwarding company.
2. **a Paischan shot:** A shot from a French nineteenth-century naval cannon more commonly spelled Paixhans.
3. **Will the N. A. Standard, and Demosthenian Shield:** The *National Anti-Slavery Standard* was a leading abolitionist newspaper, and *The Demosthenian Shield* was a Black literary newspaper published in Philadelphia. It was common at the time for newspaper editors to alert other newspapers to articles that they hoped would be reprinted.

## *Tocsin of Liberty*, August 10, 1842

1. **on the 18th ultimo:** On the eighteenth of last month.
2. **"amalgamation" or any *sich* thing:** Smallwood is dropping ribald hints about the racial "amalgamation" of children who were the product of often forced sexual relations of white male slaveholders and the women they enslaved.
3. **Oh! I see; it is the young one!:** Here and elsewhere Smallwood suggests that an enslaved boy named Henry Clay may have been fathered by, or a brother to, the Whig Party leader, U.S. senator, and Kentucky slaveholder by the same name.
4. ***Liberty day Aug. 1 '42*:** Sometimes known as Emancipation Day, August 1 marked the end of slavery in most of the British Empire in 1833 and was widely celebrated in the Caribbean, Canada, and other British territories.

## *Tocsin of Liberty*, August 24, 1842

1. **Saturday evening, the 6th instant:** On the sixth of this month.
2. **Mr. Leavitt and others, at Mrs. Sprigg's:** The abolitionist journalist Joshua Leavitt and several radical abolitionist members of Congress lived while in Washington at Mrs. Sprigg's boardinghouse.

## *Tocsin of Liberty*, August 24, 1842

1. **Your correspondent begs pardon:** Smallwood is referring to an editor's note in the previous issue of *Tocsin of Liberty*, dated

August 17, 1842, which apologized for "objectionable" passages in the previous week's "Sam Weller" letter. The editor's note did not specify what was offensive, but it may have been references to the likelihood that certain mixed-race enslaved people were the children of their enslavers, including the prominent U.S. senator Henry Clay.

## *Tocsin of Liberty*, September 7, 1842

1. **in a *werry* modest and sensible way:** Smallwood uses the eccentric spelling of "very" here and elsewhere to indicate the Cockney accent of Charles Dickens's character Sam Weller, Jr.
2. **one of my *old and intimate friends*, the Rev. C.T. Torrey:** Smallwood refers to Charles Turner Torrey, the Massachusetts-born abolitionist who had moved to Washington in late 1841 and helped Smallwood start to organize escapes from slavery. Torrey left Washington in August 1842 and began working in October 1842 as the editor of *Tocsin of Liberty*, printing and sometimes commenting on Smallwood's "Sam Weller" dispatches.
3. **as Mrs. Child says:** The reference is to the abolitionist writer and woman's rights activist Lydia Maria Child (1802–1880).
4. **Peter is out of your grasp, Mr. Clerk:** Smallwood refers to slaveholder James Larned's post as chief clerk at the Treasury Department.
5. ***to stir up the mob against the Rev. C. T. TORREY*:** Smallwood does not name the instigator, but he refers to Torrey's visit as a journalist to a slaveholders' convention in Annapolis in January 1842. Torrey was thrown out of the convention, a proslavery mob gathered around him, and a magistrate jailed him, evidently for his own protection. He was not charged with a crime.
6. **writ of fieri facias:** A court order directing the seizure and sale of property for payment of a debt.

## *Tocsin of Liberty*, November 3, 1842

1. **safe out of the hands of the Philistines!:** Smallwood is referring to Charles Torrey's departure from Washington to begin a new job as editor of *Tocsin of Liberty* in Albany. His reference to "my father" is a recurring quip about Tony Weller, the father of Samivel Weller in Dickens's *Pickwick Papers*.
2. **that Samivel Weller, jr., and Abel Brown are neither kith, kin, nor acquaintance:** Smallwood here takes pains to say the writer

hidden behind the "Samivel Weller, Jr.," pen name is neither Abel Brown, an Albany cleric and antislavery writer whose pieces often ran in *Tocsin of Liberty*, nor the Massachusetts-born Charles Torrey, as the slaveholder Azariah Fuller had evidently speculated, but an "old settler" in Washington, D.C.

3. **peck of trouble among the Patriarchs:** Smallwood's ironic term for the slaveholders, often portrayed with faux sympathy as suffering from the loss of their enslaved workers.
4. **Mr. JAMES MAHER, the public gardener:** Public gardener was an official federal post in the nineteenth century, assigned to oversee planting and maintenance of trees and shrubbery on the capital's government property.
5. **Queen Vic's dominions:** Queen Victoria's lands—in other words, Canada, part of the British Empire, where slavery had been abolished in 1833.
6. **such abolitionists as yourself and Leavitt:** Smallwood is addressing Charles Torrey as editor of *Tocsin of Liberty* and Torrey's friend, the abolitionist journalist Joshua Leavitt. He refutes speculation that Torrey and Leavitt were aiding escapes from slavery by noting that escapes did not slow after the two abolitionists left Washington.
7. **Patten, pointing over to Mrs. ——'s:** The police constable was referring to Mrs. Padgett's boardinghouse, where Charles Torrey had stayed while living in Washington. In a footnote he added to Smallwood's dispatch, Torrey claims constable Patten is lying about having issued a warrant for his arrest.
8. **Suit, Thorn and other wretches like them:** Smallwood names well-known Washington police officers who spent much of their time trying to catch and return people who escaped from slavery, collecting the ample rewards slaveholders offered.
9. **"Their eyes are holden":** Smallwood is quoting the King James Version of the Bible, Luke 24:16, which describes how Jesus returned after his crucifixion and walked beside his disciples, who did not recognize him: "But their eyes were holden that they should not know him."
10. **That name was given to it by constable ZELL of Baltimore:** In his dispatch published on August 10, 1842, Smallwood had quoted an unnamed police constable as having quipped that the large number of people escaping slavery must have gotten away on an underground railroad. Here he identified the constable as John Zell, who served in the Baltimore police force but also ran his own private detective agency and was well-known for trying to catch runaways.

11. **the great Slaveholders' Convention at Annapolis:** Maryland slaveholders gathered in the state capital in January 1842, and Torrey tried to cover the proceedings as a journalist. But he was expelled from the convention, chased by a violent mob, and eventually jailed by a magistrate, partly for his own protection.
12. **Boz DICKENS, in his new work on America:** Charles Dickens, known by the nickname Boz, had just published *American Notes for General Circulation*, an account of his recent travels in the United States, in which the British writer lambasted the institution of slavery. Smallwood's comment about "our biography" (*The Pickwick Papers*) is sarcastic; he embraced and admired Dickens's scathing views of slaveholding and the slave trade.

## *Tocsin of Liberty*, November 17, 1842

1. **Joshua Weller and Co.:** It is unknown whether "Joshua Weller," the purported nephew of "Samivel Weller, Jr.," Smallwood's pseudonym, was in fact the pseudonym of another antislavery activist. The specificity of his location in Pittsburgh, and the details about his activity aiding people escaping from slavery, might suggest a real-life counterpart.
2. **shout "*stuboy!*":** A command given to a dog to attack.
3. **the escape of several men from Williams' Pen:** The private slave jail, or pen, run by William H. Williams, Washington's leading slave trader, located just off the national mall.
4. **follow the example of the Bashaw of Tunis, and destroy the slave barracoons:** Ahmed I Bey, the ruler of Tunis in North Africa, had closed the slave market there in August 1841. A barracoon was a barracks for the enslaved.
5. **declaration of sentiments, in 1833:** This passage refers to the New York newspaper publisher William Leete Stone and his correspondent James Frederick Otis, who had signed the antislavery Declaration of Sentiments, drafted by the abolitionist William Lloyd Garrison in 1833, but who later broke with Garrison.

## *Tocsin of Liberty*, December 1, 1842

1. **Messrs. Slade, Giddings, Crafts and other boarders at Mrs. Sprigg's:** Rep. William Slade, Jr., of Vermont, Rep. Joshua Reed Giddings of Ohio, and Sen. Samuel Crafts of Vermont were among the antislavery congressmen who resided at Mrs. Sprigg's boardinghouse in Washington.

2. **But I *did* call on Mrs. SUSAN HOLMEAD:** *The Washington Directory and Governmental Register* for 1843 lists a boardinghouse run by "Mrs. Holmead" on Pennsylvania Avenue Southeast, between 3rd and 4th Streets.
3. **to pass *sub silentio*:** To pass in silence, to go without remark.
4. **to Esq. Fendall:** Philip R. Fendall II, the successor to Francis Scott Key as the United States attorney for the District of Columbia.
5. **it might be called "Blue Plains":** Blue Plains was the name of a neighborhood on the Eastern Branch, now the Anacostia River.

## *Tocsin of Liberty*, December 8, 1842

1. **the 10th article of Lord Ashburton's treaty:** The Webster–Ashburton Treaty, signed by the United States and Great Britain in 1842, called for the extradition of people charged with certain serious crimes, including robbery.
2. **President Tyler felt a *natural* anxiety about his two *almost* white sons:** The journalist Joshua Leavitt had written in 1841 that President John Tyler was the father of two young men he enslaved, named John Tyler and Charles Tyler. See https://www.presidentjohntylersenslavedhouseholds.com/tyler-paternity.
3. **Calhoun and others in the secrets of the slaveholder's plans:** Proslavery South Carolina politician John C. Calhoun, then serving as U.S. senator from South Carolina.
4. **Gerrit Smith, A. Stewart, Joshua Leavitt:** Gerrit Smith was a New York businessman and philanthropist who generously supported the antislavery cause. Alvin Stewart was an abolitionist lawyer and political candidate in New York. Joshua Leavitt was an antislavery journalist.

## *Tocsin of Liberty*, December 15, 1842

1. **sympathy with the *locofocracy*:** Smallwood uses this comical term for the Locofocos, a faction of the Democratic Party.
2. **the famous AUXILIARY GUARD:** The Auxiliary Guard was a new police unit created by Congress in Washington, D.C., in August 1842 to combat nighttime disorder. Smallwood believed it quickly came to spend most of its time and energy harassing Black people, both free and enslaved, with an eye to collecting fines and rewards.
3. **Dr. Jones, the P. M.:** The postmaster.

4. **the chairman, Hon. Mr. BRIGGS:** George N. Briggs, a Massachusetts congressmen.
5. **Messrs. Adams, Gates, Giddings, Slade, Ramsay:** All antislavery members of Congress, whom Smallwood suggests would police the Post Office. Edward Stanly, mentioned next (and misspelled "Stanley"), was a slaveholder, but Smallwood evidently had some respect for his integrity.

## *Albany Weekly Patriot*, April 27, 1843 (first of two dispatches)

1. **HENRY CHASE thanks his Boss for robbing him of *only* $4,832:** Presumably this is a rough calculation of what Henry Chase might have been paid by his enslaver had he been a free man.
2. **the amiable assistant P. M. General:** Postmaster General.

## *Albany Weekly Patriot*, April 27, 1843 (second of two dispatches)

1. **our friend, Lord Palmerston:** Henry John Temple, 3rd Viscount Palmerston, had served as the British foreign secretary from 1830 to 1841.
2. **as a special favor to *his* aristocratic American relatives:** MacTavish (as his name is usually spelled) had married into the prominent Carroll family of Maryland.
3. **the "10th article" might be stretched:** See above. The tenth article of the Webster–Ashburton Treaty allowed the extradition to the United States of people in Canada charged with certain serious crimes, including robbery.
4. **fleeing *in puris naturalibus*!:** In other words, fleeing naked.
5. **Williams' *Slave Pen*, right in front of the President's House:** Slave trader William H. Williams's slave jail or slave pen was located just off the national mall, near the White House. Whether Smallwood actually accompanied Charles "Boz" Dickens to the infamous slave trader's premises during the writer's visit to Washington in 1842 is uncertain but plausible. Dickens was such a celebrity that crowds gathered everywhere he went, and he was particularly interested in learning more about the institution of slavery, which he abhorred.
6. **He forgives him his countless stripes:** In other words, the stripes left by a whipping imposed as punishment.
7. **the interest Reverdy Johnson, Esq., of Baltimore, took:** Small-

wood refers to the arrest in Annapolis, Maryland, in January 1842 of Charles Torrey, now editor of the *Albany Weekly Patriot*. Johnson, a prominent lawyer who would later represent Torrey at his 1844 criminal trial for helping with escapes from slavery, was one of several lawyers who had helped Torrey after he was jailed in 1842.

8. **Ann Page, (quite another thing from the image of beauty, life and joy, Will Shakespeare imaged:** Smallwood jocularly distinguishes the Maryland widow and enslaver from a character of the same name in Shakespeare's *The Merry Wives of Windsor*.
9. **organ of locality:** The popular nineteenth-century pseudoscience of phrenology claimed the brain included an "organ of locality" that was enlarged in travelers and people with an excellent spatial sense.

## *Albany Weekly Patriot*, May 18, 1843

1. **New Haven, (Conn.) May 15, 1843:** Smallwood's suggestion, via Sam Weller, to have been in Connecticut, like his assertion in the November 3, 1842, issue of *Tocsin of Liberty* that he had seen New Hampshire's iconic Old Man of the Mountain, is hard to prove or disprove. As a free Black man, Smallwood could have traveled north. On the other hand, as an author writing under a pseudonym, he might have taken liberties with such details.
2. **she begged at an Irish shantee:** Usually spelled *shanty*. A small, crudely built hovel or cabin.
3. **Dr. HUN's advice:** Dr. Thomas Hun was a professor of medicine at Albany Medical College. This may refer to Hun's contention that "temperate," or moderate, drinking of alcohol was not harmful.

## *Albany Weekly Patriot*, June 15, 1843

1. **near the Columbia College:** Presumably Smallwood is referring to Columbian College in Washington, today's George Washington University.
2. **those of Latimer:** George Latimer, who had fled his enslaver, James Gray, in Norfolk, Virginia, but was recaptured in Boston, was freed by a Boston judge in 1842 and remained a free man in Massachusetts.
3. **He had never read the convincing arguments of Rev. Mr. DEW:**

In his widely read defenses of slavery, Thomas Roderick Dew, then president of the College of William & Mary in Williamsburg, Virginia, argued that love bound the slave to the master just as it connected a child and parent.

4. **THOMAS AYERS, of Hartford:** Smallwood is referring to Maryland's Harford County, northeast of Baltimore.
5. **send you some of Gadsby's green peas:** Gadsby's Tavern in Alexandria, Virginia, a well-known eatery in the nineteenth century.

## *Albany Weekly Patriot*, June 22, 1843

1. **one of the notorious C——s, of Maryland:** Smallwood clearly has in mind the Carroll family, Maryland's most prominent dynasty and one of its wealthiest, whom Smallwood mentions in other dispatches as well. Why he chose to semidisguise the name is hard to say—possibly it was a joke, since he knew any Marylander reading his words would think of the Carrolls.

## *Albany Weekly Patriot*, June 29, 1843

1. **the person of JOHN CAREY:** John Cary, as his name is usually spelled, served for years as George Washington's valet or body servant. He reported his own birth as having taken place in August 1729, which would mean he was more than 113 years old at his death on June 2, 1843, in Washington, where Smallwood could have gotten to know him.

## *Albany Weekly Patriot*, August 22, 1843

1. **wrong in regard to Mr. Martin's return:** Evidently Smallwood is referring to William Martin, who had fled his enslaver, William H. Edes of Georgetown, as recounted in his dispatches in the newspapers dated December 1, 1842, and April 27, 1843. It seems that Martin had successfully escaped, then returned to his enslaver and publicly criticized the abolitionists he had met during his sojourn in the north.
2. **your Mr. Barnard:** Rep. Daniel D. Barnard of New York, a Whig Party congressman.
3. **the end of a *motive eleven feet long*:** Smallwood suggests a long whip of the kind used by the slave traders in a private slave jail.
4. **the experienced hand of Josh Staple's, or his dirty scoundrel of a pen-keeper, Jones:** Joshua Staples worked as the jailkeeper for

Washington's most notorious slave trader, William H. Williams, and Jones was presumably one of his underlings.

## *Albany Weekly Patriot*, September 12, 1843

1. **that noble letter of G. Smith's:** The reference is to Gerrit Smith, a prominent New York state philanthropist and businessman and ardent foe of slavery.

## *Albany Weekly Patriot*, October 24, 1843

1. **The Captain, Goddard:** John H. Goddard was captain of the new Auxiliary Guard, a police unit in Washington that was financed by Congress to reduce crime but that Smallwood repeatedly accused of focusing mainly on extorting money from Black residents.
2. **the Liberty party:** The nation's first explicitly antislavery political party, cofounded by Smallwood's friend and ally Charles Torrey.

## A Narrative of Thomas Smallwood

1. **No! not when Semiramis:** Queen of Assyria in the ninth century B.C.E., legendary for her beauty, wisdom, and military prowess. "Nimrod to Sardinapalus" refers to the first and last rulers of the Assyrian monarchy. The reference touches off a virtuoso display by Smallwood of his knowledge of ancient and modern history and literature, perhaps to establish his credentials for writing a memoir.
2. **with the voice of Stentor:** In Greek myth, Stentor was a herald with Greek forces during the Trojan War, responsible for delivering messages and making announcements. His voice was said to be as loud as that of fifty ordinary men.
3. **JOHN MILTON:** The quotation is from Book I of John Milton's masterpiece, *Paradise Lost*. In the early pages of his memoir, the self-educated Smallwood seems determined to put his considerable learning on display.
4. **"Nature's sweet restorer, balmy sleep":** A well-known line in Smallwood's day from the English poet Edward Young's *Night-Thoughts* (1742).
5. **that which Dr. Johnson:** Smallwood attributes a phrase describing sleep to the eminent English author, literary critic, and lexicographer Samuel Johnson (1709–1784).

6. **says Lord Brougham:** Henry Peter Brougham (1778–1868) was a British statesman who played an important role in the passage of the Slavery Abolition Act of 1833, which directed the gradual abolition of slavery in most of the British Empire.
7. **CAMPBELL:** The Scottish poet Thomas Campbell (1777–1844) was the author of the 1836 epigram comparing the stripes on the American flag to those on the bodies of the enslaved after a whipping.
8. **REVOLT OF ISLAM:** An 1818 poem by the British poet Percy Bysshe Shelley that celebrates liberty.
9. **LORD BYRON:** Smallwood quotes "The Isles of Greece," written in 1819 by the English poet George Gordon Byron (1788–1824), who died while fighting for Greek independence.
10. **PROFESSOR LONGFELLOW:** The American poet Henry Wadsworth Longfellow (1807–1882). The lines quoted are from Longfellow's 1825 poem "The Indian Hunter."
11. **"Wha sae base as be a slave":** The line from Scottish poet Robert Burns's "Scots wha hae" translates as "whoever would be so base as to be a slave." The poem, also a song, served for years as an unofficial national anthem for Scotland.
12. **Clarkson and Wilberforce:** Thomas Clarkson (1760–1846) and William Wilberforce (1759–1833) were two of the most prominent British campaigners against the slave trade and then for the abolition of slavery.
13. **so they will George Thompson:** George Donisthorpe Thompson (1804–1878) was a British antislavery activist and member of Parliament, noted for his lecture trip to the United States in 1834–35, where he often faced threats of violence from supporters of slavery. He returned to the United States following passage by Congress of the Fugitive Slave Act in 1850, which may be what prompted Smallwood to honor him in his memoir the following year.
14. **ADDRESS TO GEO. THOMPSON:** Though Smallwood does not explicitly claim authorship, this poetic tribute to Thompson appears to be Smallwood's own work. He does not name any other author; an internet search turns up only one other appearance of the poem, a reprint in a London anthology; and the language makes clear that it was composed in Canada, Smallwood's adopted home.
15. ***Julius Cæsar*:** Smallwood's quotation is not from the Roman emperor but from Shakespeare's play about him.
16. **Mr. Paola Brown, of Hamilton:** Smallwood was evidently outraged that Brown, a Black activist in Hamilton, not far from To-

ronto, had published an antislavery pamphlet in February 1851 that copied most of its text without attribution from a famous earlier pamphlet, "An Appeal to the Colored Citizens of the World," by the Black Massachusetts activist David Walker (1796–1830). Some historians believe Brown, born in Pennsylvania in 1807, had also invented an early life in slavery. (See John Weaver's article on Paola Brown in *Dictionary of Canadian Biography*, vol. VIII.) Smallwood reprints the preface to Walker's *Appeal* and a short biography of Walker by the abolitionist and educator Henry Highland Garnet in order to bolster his accusation of plagiarism against Brown.

17. **'Saw in death his eyelids close':** The oft-quoted lines are from the poem "Marco Bozzaris" by Fitz-Greene Halleck, a tribute to a hero of the Greek war for independence.
18. **this I am prepared to prove:** Smallwood's somewhat testy preface suggests that he felt he was the victim of false rumors spread by others and wanted to set the record straight. Given that he has just accused another Black Canadian, Paola Brown, of plagiarism, he insists that his memoir is his own work and is strictly factual. Having evidently been accused of profiteering off those he helped to liberate from slavery, he also emphasizes his hard work (as a saw manufacturer) and his continuing financial contributions to the welfare of fugitives from bondage.
19. **in the clerk's office of that county:** The manumission document Smallwood refers to, dated February 14, 1815, is still on file in Maryland's digitized land records (JRM 16, p. 0297). Either Ferguson or the Prince George's County court clerk appears to have misconstrued Smallwood's age. If Smallwood was born on February 22, 1801, as he writes, he would have been thirteen years old when Ferguson filed the manumission document, not fifteen as the document states. He would have turned thirty on February 22, 1831, not February 12, 1830, as the manumission claims. Whether Smallwood or Ferguson later noticed the error is uncertain, but if Ferguson followed the document, Smallwood may have officially gained his freedom about a year ahead of schedule.
20. **the Rev. J. B. Ferguson:** The Rev. John Bell Ferguson, who had married a cousin, Sarah Ferguson, in 1808, worked at a lumberyard, presided at marriages, and did charitable work with the poor. For more on the Fergusons and Smallwood's early life, see Scott Shane, *Flee North*, chapter 1.
21. **about a year from that time I married:** Judging by the 1830 date

set by the manumission document, Smallwood would have been hired out starting in 1825 and would have married in 1826. Court records list the marriage of Thomas Smallwood and Elizabeth Anderson in 1836 ("District of Columbia Marriages, 1811–1950," familysearch.org). They may have been legally or practically unable to register their marriage while Thomas was still enslaved, so they did so a decade later.

22. **a walking curiosity in the village where I then lived:** Smallwood then lived with the Fergusons in Bladensburg, Maryland, about six miles northeast of the U.S. Capitol on the Eastern Branch, now known as the Anacostia River.

23. **Mr. John McLeod:** McLeod was a leading Washington, D.C., educator for many years, founding and operating several academies. See Shane, *Flee North*, pp. 16–18.

24. **I thought the object of that Society:** Smallwood refers to the American Colonization Society (though he calls it the African Colonization Society), which founded the republic of Liberia in West Africa and encouraged free African Americans to move there. Smallwood shifted from support for colonization to fierce opposition after coming to understand that wealthy slaveholders were among the major funders of the movement.

25. **James Brown, and a Mr. McGill:** James E. Brown trained as a pharmacist and opened an apothecary shop in Liberia with the support of the American Colonization Society. Samuel Ford McGill grew up partly in Liberia and returned to the United States to attend Dartmouth College and become the first Black medical school graduate in the country. See Gregory Bond's two-part article "Love Him and Let Him Go," *Pharmacy in History* 60, no. 3 (2018), pp. 77–88, and no. 4, pp. 124–41; and Susan Green, "Grit and Determination," *Dartmouth Medicine*, Spring 2020.

26. **the Idol of Massachusetts, Daniel Webster, the great apostate:** Webster represented New Hampshire in the U.S. House of Representatives and later Massachusetts in both the House and Senate and served twice as secretary of state. Smallwood refers to Webster's central role in the passage and enforcement of the Fugitive Slave Act of 1850, which required northerners to assist in the return of people who had escaped slavery to their enslavers.

27. **Rev. C. T. Torrey, made his appearance in Washington:** Charles Turner Torrey (1813–1846) moved to Washington at the end of 1841 to serve as Washington correspondent for a number of abolitionist newspapers in the north. His most sensational story, it

turned out, was about his own arrest and jailing after he was expelled from a convention of slaveholders in Annapolis, Maryland, and was threatened by a proslavery mob.

28. **the praise of the lady with whom he boarded:** Smallwood refers to the proprietor of Torrey's boardinghouse on 13th Street N.W. in Washington, whose last name was Padgett. As Smallwood notes, Elizabeth Smallwood had a laundry business and did the wash for Mrs. Padgett's boardinghouse.

29. **Mr. Badger of North Carolina, a Cabinet Minister:** George Edmund Badger had been appointed secretary of the navy by President William Henry Harrison, but he had resigned in September 1841. At the time Smallwood and Torrey were discussing the possible escape of some of Badger's household slaves, he had just left office but remained in Washington.

30. **monstrous, that the slaveholder should be deprived of his slaves without pay:** Smallwood in the passage that follows makes the case for aiding escapes from slavery, refuting the arguments not only of slaveholders but of some abolitionists against the radical step of violating the law by depriving enslavers of their legal property. Such abolitionists preferred to raise money to buy the freedom of the enslaved. But like Torrey, Smallwood saw no logic in compensating slaveholders for the loss of enslaved workers when those workers had never themselves been paid for their labor. He also notes that abolitionists' money would liberate far more people from bondage if they paid only the costs of escape rather than actually purchasing those people on the slave market.

31. **Patriot of this City:** Smallwood refers to the *Toronto Patriot*, published in the Canadian city from 1840 to 1852.

32. **the mode of our operations:** By Smallwood's interesting description, the first "place of deposit" or safe house would have been in or near Baltimore, where his ally Jacob Gibbs lived. The second would have been near the Susquehanna River, the first big geographical barrier on the way north. The third night's travel would have taken the fugitives into the free state of Pennsylvania.

33. **One man, by name Gunnell:** The slaveholding Washington physician Dr. William H. Gunnell was a favorite target for Smallwood's commentary and mockery, both in his newspaper dispatches and in his memoir.

34. **if I was a traitor to my brethren:** Smallwood repeatedly defends his conduct, saying he took risks and made sacrifices to organize escapes and never profited off them. The suggestion is that he had been wrongly accused, probably in Toronto's small and

sometimes contentious Black community, of exploiting freedom seekers for his own benefit. Smallwood refers to such claims against him in his extensive account of betrayals that follows. Such accusations, evidently baseless, were undoubtedly a motive for Smallwood to publish this memoir.

35. **Had I been a Physiognomist:** Physiognomy was a popular pseudoscience in the nineteenth century, now long discredited, that involved judging people's character and ability from examining their physical appearance, especially their faces.

36. **my friend G. in Baltimore:** Smallwood refers here and elsewhere to Jacob Gibbs, a Baltimore housepainter who became his trusted partner in organizing escapes. Gibbs later moved to New York City, where he remained active in helping fugitives from slavery.

37. **the eastern branch of the Potomac:** The Eastern Branch is today called the Anacostia River, which flows into the Potomac not far from Smallwood's old neighborhood near the Navy Yard.

38. **the ringing of the bell for ten o'clock:** In both Washington and Baltimore, African Americans—free as well as enslaved—were not permitted to be on the streets after 10:00 p.m.

39. **a preacher, by name Abraham Cole:** In 1833, Smallwood had been a founder along with Abraham Cole, the first minister, of the Wesley Metropolitan African Methodist Episcopal Zion Church on West D Street in Washington, often called the Wesley African Society for short. In early 1841 the two men clashed, and Smallwood denounced Cole, evidently for sexual impropriety and a passive attitude toward the slavery issue. Their dispute divided the congregation and led to the expulsion of Smallwood and an ally, Israel Wallace, in March 1841, which was chronicled in attacks and counterattacks published in local newspapers. (See, for example, letters published in *The Sun*, January 20, February 24, March 1, and March 22, 1842.) That December Smallwood sued Cole, accusing him of slander and a deliberate attempt to undermine his shoemaking business.

40. **in consequence of his improper walk:** "Improper walk" appears to be a biblical phrase meaning bad behavior, from several uses by St. Paul, often to condemn sexual misconduct. In Ephesians 4:17–19, Paul urges his followers "that ye henceforth walk not as other Gentiles walk, in the vanity of their mind . . . who being past feeling have given themselves over unto lasciviousness." Similarly, in Romans 13:13–14, Paul says, "Let us walk honestly, as in the day; not in rioting and drunkenness, not in chambering and wantonness."

41. **how different were my feelings that day:** Smallwood's remarks about his feelings about being on British soil on American Independence Day prefigure the famous speech Frederick Douglass would give nine years after Smallwood first reached Toronto and a year after Smallwood published his memoir. Douglass's address, "What to the Slave Is the Fourth of July?," was delivered on July 5, 1852, to the Rochester Ladies' Anti-Slavery Society in Rochester, New York.
42. **by the watch, and Goddard, their Captain at their head:** Smallwood refers to the city's Auxiliary Guard, headed by John Goddard. Smallwood had earlier recounted the same event, omitting Goddard's use of his name, in a dispatch for the *Albany Weekly Patriot*, October 24, 1843, printed in this book.
43. **through the kindness of Mr. Pitman:** Smallwood is probably referring to the Baltimore dry-goods merchant Edward Pittman. It is unclear whether Thomas or Elizabeth Smallwood knew Pittman from some earlier encounter or whether she randomly encountered him that day and explained the family's predicament.
44. **Messrs. Croker, Thomson and Latimore, of Albany, N. Y.:** Smallwood is likely referring to George L. Crocker, a white antislavery activist who ran a horse livery service; Richard Thompson, a Black abolitionist and member of the antislavery Albany Vigilance Committee; and Benjamin Lattimore, Jr., a grocer and prosperous businessman who was a member of one of Albany's most prominent African American families.
45. **a defunct institution, got up by a few designing persons:** Smallwood refers to the Dawn settlement in Canada, north of Lake Erie, where a community of African Americans who had escaped slavery had settled. At an 1847 gathering of Black leaders in Drummondville, Canada, Smallwood confronted Josiah Henson, one of the founders of Dawn and the supposed model for Uncle Tom in Harriet Beecher Stowe's *Uncle Tom's Cabin*, and accused him of pocketing money donated to Dawn for the support of Black refugees. (In the original text of Smallwood's *Narrative*, "Dawn" is spelled "Don.")
46. **Mr. Paine, a preacher of the same denomination:** The Rev. Daniel A. Payne was a prominent bishop of the African Methodist Episcopal Church and a colleague of the Rev. William Nichols, whom Smallwood mentions above. In his 1891 *History of the African Methodist Episcopal Church* (p. 176), Payne claims that Nichols had assisted Charles Torrey in helping organize escapes from slavery.

47. **that excellent gentleman's, Mr. Thomas Garrett's:** Thomas Garrett (1789–1871) was a wealthy Wilmington, Delaware, businessman and antislavery activist, known for helping many people fleeing slavery on their way north.
48. **we put out for Kennett Square:** The original reads "Gannet's Square," but there is no such town, and it appears to be an imprecise phonetic rendering of Kennett Square.
49. **Mr. Hall, a lawyer:** David A. Hall (1795–1870), though for a time opposed to outright abolition of slavery, became a prominent antislavery lawyer in Washington, representing both people in slavery and those helping them escape.
50. **the first issue of the Baltimore Sun:** *The Sun* ran its story on November 27, 1843, attributing the account to John Goddard, captain of the Auxiliary Guard. It was the first newspaper article to name Thomas Smallwood as an organizer of escapes, and it was widely reprinted.
51. **because Capt. Richardson:** Capt. Hugh Richardson (1784–1870) owned and operated a steamship on Lake Ontario for many years. He sent his sons to the prestigious Upper Canada College, where Smallwood's son William studied, and it appears the two men were friendly acquaintances. See the entry on Richardson in *Dictionary of Canadian Biography*, online edition.
52. **by the passage of that iniquitous fugitive law:** Smallwood is referring to the Fugitive Slave Act of 1850, which strengthened the requirement that federal government officials in the north assist in the return to slavery of people who had escaped bondage and increased penalties for anyone interfering in the return of runaways.
53. **superintendent of the government grounds, attached to the President's house:** Smallwood refers to James Maher, whom he discusses in his dispatch to the November 3, 1842, edition of *Tocsin of Liberty*, printed above.
54. **if they refuse to repent in the day of grace that is given them to follow after righteousness, Jer. viii. 20:** Smallwood, a religious man who was sometimes identified in his Toronto years as "the Rev. Thomas Smallwood," offers a series of Bible passages to support his conclusion that the United States would be punished by God for the crime of slavery.
55. **attempted to expel from their hall a servant of God, the Hon. Mr. Seward:** Smallwood appears to be referring to a failed proposal to expel from the Senate William H. Seward, then a U.S. senator from New York, for his opposition to the proslavery elements of the Compromise of 1850, including the Fugitive Slave Act.

56. **the infamous traffic of slave breeding and trading among themselves:** While it is difficult to confirm the numbers cited by Smallwood, his account is consistent with later scholars' study of the domestic slave trade that arose after Congress banned the import of captive Africans in 1808. There is a rough consensus that about one million enslaved people were forced from the upper south to the deep south between about 1810 and the Civil War, three quarters of them through middlemen operating as slave traders.
57. **the supineness of the United States Naval Officers in suppressing the African slave trade:** Scholars have confirmed Smallwood's contention that the United States Navy was generally inactive or timid in enforcing the ban on the African slave trade. British ships were far more active in enforcing the ban.
58. **Senator Knight, of Rhode Island:** Nehemiah Rice Knight (1780–1854), a former Rhode Island governor, represented the state in the U.S. Senate from 1821 to 1841.
59. **many of their descendants in Nova Scotia:** Some enslaved African Americans who left their enslavers and fought with the British in the Revolutionary War and the War of 1812 were rewarded by British authorities with plots of land in Nova Scotia.
60. **the Queen's Bush:** A large tract of land on British territory in what is today southwestern Ontario in which several communities were formed after 1820 by Black settlers, many of them formerly enslaved in the United States.
61. **Drummondville, C. W.:** Drummondville, the site of an early "colored convention" in 1847, is a city in Ontario, then known as Canada West.
62. **the venerable Professor Davis:** John A. G. Davis (1802–1840) was a law professor at the University of Virginia, where he was murdered by a student for taking part in the expulsion four years earlier of members of a student militia.

# ALSO AVAILABLE

## THE MIS-EDUCATION OF THE NEGRO

**Introduction by Jarvis R. Givens**

Carter G. Woodson identified a relationship between distortions of Black life in curriculum and the violence circumscribing Black life in the material world. This systematic process of mis-education undermined Black people's struggles for freedom and justice, and it was an experience that scholars before and after Woodson recognized and worked to challenge.

## THE PORTABLE FREDERICK DOUGLASS

**Edited by John Stauffer and Henry Louis Gates, Jr.**

This compact volume offers the full range of Douglass's works: the complete *Narrative of the Life of Frederick Douglass*, as well as extracts from *My Bondage and My Freedom* and *Life and Times of Frederick Douglass*; *The Heroic Slave*, one of the first works of African American fiction; the speeches that launched his political career; and his wide-ranging journalism.

## TWELVE YEARS A SLAVE

**Foreword by Steve McQueen, Introduction by Ira Berlin**

*Twelve Years a Slave* is a harrowing memoir recounting how Solomon Northup, born a free man in New York, was lured to Washington, D.C., in 1841 with the promise of fast money, then brutally sold into slavery. He spent the next twelve years of his life in captivity on a Louisiana cotton plantation. After his rescue, Northup published this exceptionally vivid account.

PENGUIN CLASSICS

Ready to find your next great classic? Let us help. Visit prh.com/penguinclassics